There are many books on how to do magick, but not so many with stories about actually doing it and what happens. *NakedTantra* lays bare the inner states of the two brave souls involved in this extended magical work.

Copyright © 2020 Miryamdevi & Minanath
First edition 2020

All rights reserved. No part of this work may be reproduced or utilized in any form by any means, electronic or mechanical, including *xerography, photocopying, microfilm,* and *recording,* or by any information storage system without permission in writing from the publishers.

Naked Tantra

Record of a Magical Year

Miryamdevi
&
Minanath

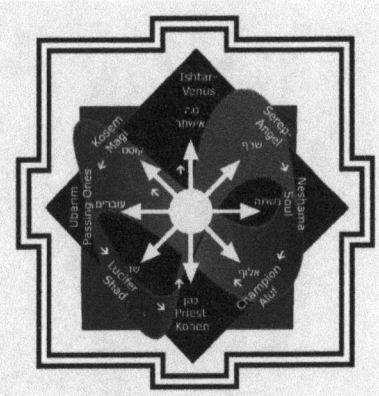

Unusual disclaimer

Of necessity the contents of this grimoire might be considered erotic. And, with that thought in mind, it might also be that the reader is occasionally aroused by our story as it progresses. Some might find this an unwanted intrusion, into what is otherwise an exploration of a magical world. Others we surmise, will take this in good part, accepting that, a spoonful of sugar helps the medicine go down. To those who do not share these sensibilities, and are unmoved by what you are about to read, we offer our sincerest apologies.

NakedTantra is intentionally rendered as a single word of eleven characters throughout this text, the wise reader will understand why.

Pantheistic Bes Statuette, late period 26th dynasty, reign of Psamtik 1, ca 664-610 BCE now in Louvre E11554

Rap to Pan

Thrill with lovely lust of the light,
O man! My man!
Come charging out of the night
Of Pan! Io Pan!
Io Pan! Io Pan! Come over the sea
From shambala and paradise !
Roaming like Bacchus, with his guards
Companion females and males all hard
On a milk-white ass, come over the sea
To me, to me!
Come with priestess in bridal dress
(Shepherdess and pythoness)
Come with Artemis, who in wildwood trod,
And wash your white thigh, beautiful god,
In the moon of the woods, on the lotus press,
The golden tongue my jewel to bless!
Dip the purple of passionate prayer
In the crimson shrine, lusty & bare,
Your soul that startles with eyes of blue
As we watch your ecstasy seeping through
The tangled thicket, the ancient grove
Of the living tree that is spirit and soul
And body and brain — come over the sea,
(Io Pan! Io Pan!)
Devil or god, to me, to me,
My man! my man!

Come with trumpets sounding shrill
Over the hill!
Come with drums low thundering
From the spring!
Come with flute and come with pipe!
Am I not ripe?
I, who wait and tremble and wrestle
With breathe that has no way to settle
My body, weary of empty embrace,
Strong as a lion and smooth as a snake —
Come, O come!
I am numb
With the lonely lust of devildom.
Thrust the sword through iron fetters,
All-devourer, all-begetter;
Give me the sign of the Open Eye,
And the token aroused of horny thigh,
And the word of madness and mystery,
O Pan! Io Pan!
Io Pan! Io Pan Pan! Pan Pan! Pan,
I am one love
Do as you will, as a great god can,
O Pan! Io Pan!
Io Pan! Io Pan Pan! I am awake
In the grip of the snake.
The eagle slashes with beak and claw;
The gods withdraw:

The great beasts come. Io Pan! I am borne
To come on the horn
Of the Unicorn.
I am Pan! Io Pan! Io Pan Pan! Pan!
I am your mate, I am your one,
Goat of your flock, I am gold, I am god,
Flesh to your bone, flower to your rod.
With hoofs of steel I race on the rocks
Through solstice sunrise to equinox.
And I rave; and I howl and I rip and I rend
Everlasting, world without end,
Maenad, Mystoi, Woman, Man,
In the might of Pan.
Io Pan! Io Pan Pan! Pan! Io Pan!
(found after AC)

Foreword

"A dream is something you see, not something you do. It's a vision, premonition or memory."
–Kasia Kzapakowski, *Behind closed eyes, dreams & nightmares in ancient Egypt*

"Magick is preparation for making love"
–Shri Mahindra

"To the orthodox Vaisnavas, as to most Christian poets, the image of love in separation and its extension, extra marital or adulterous love, was an image of the relationship of the soul to god." ...
–Edward C. Dimock, *The Place of the Hidden Moon : Erotic Mysticism in the Vaishavasahajiya Cult of Bengal* (1966).

"Erotika"

In sex, the existence of a soul may be revealed, unmediated by language, and able to converse directly, monad to monad. *The Poignancy of Old Pornography* is the title of a little film from philosopher Alain de Botton's "School of Life". We appreciate the linkage with an existential message about the fleeting quality of life. It also provides a motif and insight into NakedTantra.

Xavier Bolot's book *The Three Realities*, that is to say the physical, the perceived and the represented, provides another insight into our project. When we talk of reality we are usually thinking about encounters with the Other, that is to say the external world or even another person. Is the external world real, are the people one meets real or are they constructions of one's mind? We see each other with our visual senses and we express things in language, by speaking. But as Buddhists long ago recognised, both these things are problematic, for we do not see things as they really are, and language, which is slower than thought, can be deceptive.

In contrast, the physical body seems to just know things quicker than either of these other senses. So for example if we accidentally place our hand on a flame which would burn us, the body moves away from the heat in an instant, quicker than the eyes or brain can detect the problem.

Touching and the physical are very primary senses. The more intimate the touch, the more primary and direct is the exchange of information. Thus in NakedTantra we are to some extent, not burdened with spoken language. Once we are connected, it is our bodies that do the "communicating", lingam and yoni, they converse in their own language and in the most unexpected way. Ideally, as we explore each others ideas, as we probe the innermost secrets, literally, we are stirring the pot or cauldron, the alchemical vessel. This is the ideal, of course the connection may fail but some, hopefully we two, are blessed by moments of perfect communication.

Acknowledgments

Shri Lokanath Maharaj, Michael Kelly, SteveD who introduced us, Ana Jones who translated the Canto de Nana shown on page 93. To my friend Didi for personal accounts.

Contents

Rap to Pan 6
Foreword 9
"Erotika" 9
Acknowledgments 11

Chapter 1 Dearest Mina 15
Tantrik Symposium in The House of Red Dreams 16
The Call 16
Ganesha – the opening rite & invocation 17
Vinayaka Ahaval 3
(Invocation to the breaker of obstacles) 19
Initiation into the Dream mysteries 21
Invocation of Kundalini 23
Dhyana (Guided meditation) 24
The fivefold kiss 26
Blessing 29
The Alchemical Wedding 30
The Red Veil Mysteries… 32

Chapter 1 Prolegomena 35
How Demon Lovers meet (Breaking the Ice) 37
A First Dream Sending 42
First love making 48

Chapter 2 Baboons 58
A First Naked Tantra Session – Miryam's Initiation 59
The First Ritual (10 March) 65
Meanwhile 77
Lover's Story 77

Chapter 3 Fire and Water 80
Liber MMM 84
The Ritual 90
Lover's Story 99

Chapter 4 The Kiss of Life
Fire and water 102
Demons 104
Abramelin 106
From Grimoire of the Morgan Witches 111
Naked Tantra 3 – Kiss of Life - Mid April 121
Miryam thru the playlist: 122
The Kiss 124
The Tantrik Kiss 127
Kiss of Life Ritual (continued) 129
Lover's Story 133

Chapter 5 Behemoth, the elephant
Magical record of the Morgan witches 136
Dream control by sexual magick 151
Lover's Story 153

Chapter 6 Vampires
Vampires (from Grimoire of Morgan Witches) .. 158
Aleister Crowley Comes
  (from Grimoire of Morgan Witches) 161
More On Aleister Crowley 166
Stillness Ritual Session (19th May) 170
Lover's Story 178

Chapter 7 Transition 183
Seth, Apophis & Baphomet 184
More on ritual 188
Hippo/Tawaret, and the nature of Transition 190

Premonitory dreams 192
Ipet Invocation 194
Memories of the rite 196
Ipet ritual but from Miryam's perspective 201
The Invocation 202
The Playlist 205
Red Mage 207
"Carnal Gnosis" 210
PGM IV 154-285 – Nephotes (Khonsu) 211
Lover's Story 212

Chapter 8 Down to Earth 214
Mina to Stonehenge 215
Oxford to Stonehenge then Glastonbury 217
Stonehenge 219
The Rite 220
Glastonbury Romance 223
Brean Down 226
Friday Morning 229
Lover's Story 230
Afterword To Egypt? 234
At the Airport 235

Appendix 237
The Archaeology of Sex 237
Sexual Repression? 237
Index 240

Ganapati Temple Pune

Chapter 1
Dearest Mina

For quite some time now I have been thinking of "The Symposium"...

And now I am ready to describe how I think it will be, actually a sort of initiation into our mysteries – which I don't know how else we should call them, other than the name we most agree on and which makes us happy, the word you came up with, NakedTantra.

I dreamt of the Shakti wearing her red saree, it was so very vivid and she showed me how things should be, and I knew I had to write them down, and a few nights ago, the words began to flow, it all came out.

It is almost finished, I've written it all, and now I share it with you, my dearest lover, the most special things...

Tantrik Symposium
in The House of Red Dreams

A night time ritual and initiation into the tantrik dreaming consciousness (and subconsciousness).

The Call

People listen
People come
People listen
People, come
Come to my Sabbath
The stately pleasure zone
For Vira heroes & Devi goddesses
Whose rites have almost begun
Hear the call to adventure,
& come.
Come with a heart as light as a feather.
Come, Earth-Child to the endeavour,
& enter the path of darkness.

Where light will be extended
Khabs en pekht - Konx om pax[1]

Ganesha – the opening rite & invocation

The courtyard is buzzing with people who, almost as soon as they arrive, are hugging, kissing, eating, drinking. The whole place echoes with their laughter and excited chitchats. Soft music fills the temple. They are the mystoi, seekers of the mysteries. Inside, a shrine to elephant headed deity Ganesha is nearing completion – just one more touch of red flowers, just a few more lamps ...

Miryam-Shakti wears her translucent, red wedding saree which is just right for this night, when there will be an alchemical wedding. In any initiation, one's blood is changed to that of the tribe.[2] Her Shiva, Mina, wears his white turban, short koti and lungi. Mina & Miryam kneel at the altar before Ganesh, they burn incense and light the lamps, which add their weird glow to the already vermillion light. Each takes kumkum paste on their thumb and lovingly makes a bindi

---

1 "Konx en Pekht" is reported to be the words uttered to the initiates by the hierophant in the ancient Greek mysteries, they heard this as soon as they arrived at the entrance to the secret chamber, after a long journey through the sacred landscape. with many trials. What happened next after the initiates entered the temple and the doors closed behind them, remains one of the best kept secrets of antiquity. It is suggested that the utterance is based on an Egyptian original, "Khabs en Pekht" meaning "Light in Extension".

2 The Kula really reflects the sort of alchemical transformation that occurs with initiation, as in marriage where a woman's blood was said to change to that of the caste of her husband.

over each other's third eye. Mina-Shiva rings a little bell three times, the signal for them to vibrate the Ganesh Mantra in unison.

(https://youtu.be/6xrKeJ9unMA)

Lord Ganesha Mantra:
Om Gan Ganpataye Namo Namah
Om Gan Ganpataye Namo Namah
Om Gan Ganpataye Namo Namah

On the altar the beautiful image of Ganesha glows. Adorned with all adornments, red flowers, candles, a bowl of special round sweets, the luddoo, like embryonic thoughts, awaiting manifestation. And of course wine, lots of wine.

One by one, the mystoi enter. They kneel or sit around a four-square sanctuary, the flame red, living altar in the centre of the sacred space. Their breathing soon becoming synchronised with the vibrations of the mantra

Om Gan Ganpataye Namo Namah

The mantra ends and the room is again very quiet and still, aside from the rhythmic breathing of the participants, synchronised together as one body.

Mina priest stands and faces north and recites a Ganesha invocation in his clearest voice:

Vinayaka Ahaval[3]
(Invocation to the breaker of obstacles)

Cool fragrant lotus feet with anklets tinkling sweet,
Gold girdle, flower-soft garment setting off comely hips,
Potbelly and big, heavy tusk,
Elephant face with the bright, red mark,
Five hands, the goad, the noose,
Blue body dwelling in the heart;
Pendulous jaws, four mighty shoulders,
Three eyes and the three musk tracks,
Two ears, the gold crown gleaming,
The breast aglow with the triple thread,
O Being, bright and beautiful!
Wish-yielding elephant,
Born of the Master of Mystery in Mount Kailasa,
Mouse rider fond of the three famed fruits;
Desiring to make me yours this instant
You like a mother have appeared before me
And cut off the delusion of unending births;
Stilled my mind in tranquil calm beyond speech and thought;
Clarified my intellect,
Plunged me in bliss
which is the common ground of Light

---

3   Vinayaka Ahaval "Adoration to the Remover of Obstacles" Translated from Tamil by Tiru K. Swaminathan The Vinayagar Agaval (Song of Vinayaga) is a stunning example of Tamil sacred poetry. It is thought to be the greatest poem of the Chola era poet Auvaiyar, written shortly before her death.

And darkness;
Boundless beatitude you have given me,
Ending all affliction, show the way of grace,
Siva lingam within the heart,
Atom within atom, vast beyond all vastness!
Sweetness hid in the hardened node,
You have steadied me clear in human form all
Besmeared with holy ashes;
Added me to the congregation of your servants true
and trusty;
Made me experience in my heart the inmost meaning
of the five letters;
Restore my real state to me, and rule me now,
O Master of Wisdom, Vinayaka;
Your feet alone, Your feet alone are my sole refuge
Aum Ganesha

(https://youtu.be/iXJ38KBOm8o)

Now music, the chanting of the Svetasvatara Upanishad by Sharmila Roy, vibrates around the room, which bring us softly and gently back to the here and now.

Slowly we move into the centre.

(https://youtu.be/Yr4aRrDMQfo)

And the Shiva mantra:

Om Namah Shivayah

Miryam Shakti walks in her lovely way around the circle of the mystoi, who have taken places on their dragon seats. To each she hands a special sweet luddoo, little *cakes of light*, that hold the most sacred elixir of her essence.

In the centre of the dragon circle of the mystoi, is a bowl of ashes, the freshly burned remnants of the Fire of Azazel. Ashes to remind us that we have all already performed our own funeral, and are beyond life and death.

Initiation into the Dream mysteries

Mina-Shiva and Miryam-Shakti take their seat facing each other, the bowl of ashes, the Fire of Azazel between them. The mystoi around them are deep in meditation, reflecting on the moon, the sun and the burning fire of passion!

They know they have to focus on the rhythm of their heart as it beats

1, 2, 3, relax...
4, 5, your body is relaxed...
slowly, slowly they go deeper,
6, 7, 8, relax now and go deeper,
9, 10 ...deeper ... relax...

The tinkling of a distant bell is sweet and melodic, and draws everyone back from whence they have been, in far away lands. Shiva and Shakti stand up in one graceful movement, and gesture for the mystoi to also rise, and remain encircling them. Shiva-Shakti call out the words from a sacred text, that the mystoi will then repeat after them.

> "Nakedness shall be our freedom
> A symbol of our new way, our magical life
> It is the highest expression of creation...
> ... we seek to know more of this way of life
> We renounce shame, shyness and inhibitions

We renounce the ways of darkness and ignorance."

Shakti then lifts the bowl of ashes in her hands, and with a gentle shrug, she lets her saree fall to the ground, revealing her beautiful nakedness. She gestures that the mystoi may now do the same.

One by one they are to receive the eight marks of peace, freedom and happiness. As each comes to stand before Shiva/Shakti they hear:

I consecrate your brow to Divine Wisdom
Shiva-Shakti then marks his/her brow with ashes

I consecrate your breasts to love's embrace
Shiva-Shakti mark his/her breasts with ashes

I consecrate your genitals to the Creator's enjoyment
Shiva-Shakti mark his/her genitals with ashes

I consecrate your hands to eternal service
Shiva-Shakti mark his/her hands with ashes
I consecrate your feet to walk our path
Shiva-Shakti mark his/her feet with ashes
The rite is complete
We honour the triple-natured Goddess
We honour the Lord of awareness
Peace – freedom – happiness to all ...

The first ritual ends and there is an interlude. Everyone remains in the temple where there are refreshments, wine, beer, and other mind altering substances.

> The Hare Krishna mantra is heard:
> Hare Krishna, Hare Krishna
> Krishna Krishna, Hare Hare
> Hare Rama, Hare Rama
> Rama Rama, Hare Hare
>
> (https://youtu.be/VP623hMbAIA)

Mina & Miryam, using their foreknowledge and intuition, take the opportunity in this time, to ask people to become mindful of their partners for what follows, and stay close and in contact with them for the next part of the rite.

Invocation of Kundalini

The Kreem Kali Mantra is heard :

> Om Kreem Kalikayai Namah
>
> (https://youtu.be/5kwCANKHYh4)

While the Kali mantra starts, Mina and Miryam return to their places standing adjacent to the dunni (ashpit). The mystoi, in their couples, approach their dragon mats.

Mina and Miryam gesture for the mystoi to lie down on their mats in shivasana (death pose), and listen with all the care they of course possess, letting the words of the mantra flow through them.

Dhyana (Guided meditation)

Uttered by Miryam:

Close your eyes and focus on your breath – in from your nose and out through your mouth.
Relax your feet, your legs, your buttocks, your abdomen.
Release your lower back, relax your pelvis,
Feel the muscles along your spine relaxing,
Your shoulders and arms are relaxed;
Your neck, head and face are relaxed.
Keep breathing
In & out, in & out.
Your body sinks into the ground, into the earth.
Tendrils are growing out from your body. You are rooted in the earth now, and from it other tendrils grow up, to connect with you.
All the while you are breathing steadily,
In, and out, in, and out.
You feel the roots vibrating around you with the rhythm of your breath, pulsating, slowly, as they wind and coil around you. They are soft and cool on your skin.
Something is stirring in you, gently uncoiling and moving up through your legs, moving along your spine, around your heart, back down to your solar plexus, and returning to its sacred seat, at the root of the yoni lingam. You feel it swaying inside you, as you move with the rhythm of the mantra.
Slowly, slowly, you sit up, your body still swaying to the rhythm of the mantra.

She has awakened,
Growing within you.
She rises in peace.
You keep swaying
Feel her stretching her long, sinuous snake-like body.
She unravels in your back, your spine, she moves to
the enchanting rhythm.
Lift your arms, touch your face.
Touch your head and feel your body.
Swaying still, now stand.
Slow dancing with the serpent goddess.
She, who is within you.
Feel how she moves through your spine,
Moves through your neck,
Until, she comes to rest,
Her eyes behind your eyes, looking out.
Open your eyes,
and look out, with those of kundalini.
Look around, look for your partner,
See them, go to them,
Dance with them.

The mantra fades & comes to its end.
You, the mystoi, still swaying,
Just a little longer,
Until the motion becomes gentle and easy,
You and your partner, facing and one.

Hear the words of Miryam and Mina:
Fine as a fiber of lotus stalk, She is the Goddess Maya (of

uncanny power), who bewilders the created. She covers the mouth of the phallic stone with her own mouth and is coiled around it three and a half times, like a sleeping snake. Her murmur sounds like the drone of innumerable intoxicated bees.

The Five fold kiss

The Goddess chant begins

Isis Astarte Diana Hecate Demeter Kali Inanna

(https://www.youtube.com/watch?v=hHAhA3cSLIE)

While the goddess chant is playing, take your partner's hand, as Mina takes Miryam's, and lead them to your dragon seat, as he leads her to the red veil altar.

Together they stand before the altar. Miryam is almost naked, apart from her red saree, which covers her head and face like a wedding veil.

Mina wears his white Tallit over his shoulders, as a shawl.

As Mina speaks to Miryam, so shall the mystoi speak one to another, as he does, so shall you do with your partner.

Blessed be your feet that have brought you in your ways.

[Kisses both feet]

Blessed be your knees that shall kneel at the sacred altar

[Anoints and kisses both knees]

Blessed be your yoni that gives us life

[Anoints and kisses the yoni]

Mina stands and cups Miryam's breasts in his hands and says:
Blessed be your breasts, formed in beauty, to sustain us in this life

> [Anoints and kisses both breasts]

Mina lifts the red veil from Miryam's face and says:
Blessed be your lips, that utter the sacred names

> [Kisses her lips]

As Miryam speaks to Mina, so shall the mystoi speak one to another, as she does, so shall you do with your partner.

Now, Mina is standing, his Tallit[4] rearranged so it covers his head. Miryam is kneeling at his feet.

Blessed be your feet that have brought you in your ways.

> [Anoints and kisses both feet]

Blessed be your knees that shall kneel at the sacred altar.

> [Anoints and kisses both knees]

Blessed be your lingam that gives us life.

> [Anoints and kisses the lingam]

---

4   The Tallit Miryam gave Mina is 100cm x 150cm. Many years ago in Glastonbury, during my initiation practice, I saw an image of the portable shrine, white muslin stretched across poles to make a tao shaped tent - a canopy (chuppa) floated over it. My "father" was inside, a voice told me to go in and see him. As I did the light floating above it sank down and filled it with gnosis

Miryam stands and touches Mina's breast with her hands and says:
Blessed be your breast, formed in strength, to protect us in this life

[Anoints and kisses both breasts]

Miryam stands to bless Mina's lips. She comes under his Tallit, blessing his lips with her lips. Under the Tallit with him, blessing his lips, they keep kissing.

All are now kissing, as Tantrikas do.

Blessing

Kneeling by the altar
Naked
Blessing and kissing my feet
my knees
Blessing my yoni and kissing it
I can feel your tongue searching
Licking
The jewel in the lotus is so bright
The serpent is awake
Spiraling up my spine
Hissing to a strange rhythm
Fully erect you bless my breast
and suck my nipples
Licking my lips
and kissing them gently
Our tongues dance
The sacred dance
Electricity surging down my spine
We kiss
The kiss of life

The Alchemical Wedding

Standing under moonlit sky and shining stars
A Tallit of white and silver
A canopy of lights
You put Ganesha on my finger
And whisper in my ear -
Time to kneel by the altar
My dear
Kissing the feet of the
Ancient priest
Marking his knees with my lips
I take Apep in my mouth
His eye glistened and moist
For a moment or two
We are lost in the void
You help me back
To my feet
Your eyes
Your eyes
Your eyes
Like two shining scarabs
Staring into my soul
Sharing a secret
I recall
The moon priest
Holds me tight in his arms
While I kiss his chest
and bless his heart
Under the Tallit of silvery lights
Our lips met
A kiss and a breath

Leonard cohen – dance me to the end of love
Oh let me see
Your beauty when
the witnesses are gone
Let me feel you moving
Like they do in Babylon
Show me slowly what
I only know the limits of
Oh ...dance me
To the end of love

(https://youtu.be/2zjLBWnZGTU)

The Red Veil Mysteries...

(Based on the dream of the 'Red Shakti')

The room is suffused with the gentle red light of several lanterns, incense smoke hangs in the air, so thick one can almost taste it along with heady scent of perfumes, the sacred oils.

The excitement in the room is tangible.

Mina & Miryam begin the chanting of the Mantra

Lam - LLAAAAAMMMMM

The mystoi, the adepts, who are there to witness and participate in the spectacle anew, form their crescent around them, and as the mantra progresses, they go deeper & deeper, until they each relax and lie down.

Mina takes Miryam's hand and leads her through the translucent red veil that encloses a central sanctuary, which is also an altar.

The mantra continues to vibrate through her body and she can feel her beloved's is vibrating too.

Her heart is racing, what are we going to do next? They never really discussed it, they always said that when the time will come they will know what to do, but do they, do we?

Mina closes the red muslin curtains of the sanctuary altar. In one graceful movement, Miryam lies down and arranges her wonderful body on it in anticipation, for this is also a beautiful great bed, with soft red fabric, lush skins, furs and great cushions.

As Shakti she lies there, her red saree barely covering her

beautiful body. She smiles a smile at her Mina and says to him, in a voice just audible to the company:

… Come

The words of the ancient prayer:

"I love you! I yearn to you! Pale or purple, veiled or voluptuous, I, who am all pleasure and purple, and drunkenness of the innermost sense, desire you. Put on the wings, and arouse the coiled splendour within you: come unto me!"

Mina, now as Shiva, kneels down before her. He takes her feet in his hands and kisses them gently. Lovingly. He continues massaging and rubbing her ankles. Miryam, as goddess Kameshvari is vibrating with ecstasy.

Mina kisses her knees, then caresses her thighs, and finally he parts her legs, so her beautiful yoni, is revealed.

Mina's lungi is now as loose as Miryam's saree, his lingam rises free. And he knows, for Miryam has told him, she has a space inside her for him. And she will open for him, and the union of Mina's lingam and Miryam's yoni is just perfect for their love and bliss.

Kneeling before her, as at the divine altar, he sees the fruit of Daath, right there for him to touch, to kiss, to lick, to taste.

The pulse of the Shakti is guiding him to her, to that most exquisite exotic flower, moistened with the amrita nectar of blue lilies. Sweet like honey, he hears the droning of lovesick bees in his ears. He tastes, one little kiss… before his lips are around her tiny erected djed jewel. His tongue soft and wet gliding, dancing, exploring.

Yes, kiss my yoni she says, her voice is so lovely, entranced. As in a dream you kiss, you lick, you suck, you fuck.

Shakti is shaking, vibrating, humming.

Come to me she says, Come, and again with the words of an ancient song "To me! To me! Sing the rapturous love-song unto me! Burn to me perfumes! Wear to me jewels! Drink to me, for I love you!

I love you!"

The fruit of knowledge is indeed intoxicating. Miryam is one deep languid, orgasmic pool. And Mina at last must plunge into her, burying himself in his beloved goddess. Their lust, endless, as she takes him inside, enfolding, encircling and grasping him as he grasps her, so tight, their union, their kundalini, in the moment, eternal.

Now they cannot separate, wrapped as they are in each other's dream. Will they, sooner or later, as you'd think they must, their ecstasy pause, if only for the briefest of interludes, so the story can begin. As long ago, the earth god Geb withdrew after his centuries of coupling with star goddess Nwt, pushed apart by those who see. So they sit, blinking at each other, strangely content, looking, each on each, smiling, the flush of love still on them … the sweet perfume of sweat in their nostrils, as all about them sleep & dream, as you who read this must also dream.

Chapter 1
Prolegomena

Mina means "Introduction"
"The guru invokes the dream mantra in order that
they [the disciples] have visions in their sleep."
—Siddhanta-shekhara tantra

Well I guess, one way or another, that's what happened at the Red Saree rite. So the "...mystoi are effortlessly initiated,

---

Agathon Demon or perhaps Renenutet/Meretseger,
"she who loves silence", Cairo museum.

without the aid of external gurus or masters, by their own divinized powers of cognition, called 'yoginis'."

That's more or less a quote from David Gordon White's writing about High Hindu Tantra. In this case I think we can include you, gentle reader, as you progress through this text, if you want it that way.

Back in the day, the tantric way was more earthy, although it seems like the path then was a middle one, a blend of internal and external powers, doing the work.

Magicians of the past, and indeed of the present, live in a complex universe, where they encounter supernatural entities, such as the yoginis, in their Mind, which could be in waking life or in dreams. They also meet them through, or is it in, another person?

The original magick of India got toned down a lot as time progressed. But there are still plenty of examples to be found of the more adventurous adepts. Thus "in early south Indian history ... women could unabashedly be erotically possessed by Murugan, ... it was with the development of brahmanical Hinduism in south India, that it was inconceivable for a god to reside in the (supposedly) 'impure female vessel' ." How wrong they were about that. Note, that the name of the god in this passage, Murugan, is so close to another name that figures in what follows.[1]

---

1. Obeyesekere, Gananath. *Medusa's Hair: An Essay on Personal Symbols and Religious Experience.* Chicago ; London: U of Chicago, 1981. p151

How Demon Lovers meet
(Breaking the Ice)
16th-17th February

Breaking the ice, that would be Miryam's doing, though she wasn't Miryam when she did it. This would be 17th February – just two days after the new moon, at an Occult Conference in Glastonbury.

In this incarnation they met in the flesh for the first time at the previous year's occult conference. Mina was leading a workshop on Egyptian Spirit Dance. After this Miryam found Mina on facebook and they maintained a sporadic friendship via social media.

Thinking back, Mina remembered being aware of Miryam's presence even then, there was something about her. Breakfasting in a coffeeshop, just two among others from the conference, on the Sunday morning, enjoying the time, well perhaps enjoying is an exaggeration. They shared a table but didn't speak directly. Mina caught himself thinking about her, thinking to himself, Miryam is very attractive, but then he remembered she had introduced herself with her sister-in-law, so she must be married, loved by another. He put the thought that there was, or could be any mutual attraction, out of his mind.

When they met again after a year of occasional messages and shared ideas, Mina was still wondering, secretly hoping. He arrived at his lodging in Glastonbury, almost immediately he received a message from Miryam. She was in such and such a restaurant, why didn't Mina join her? He showered and got there just in time for food. Miryam seemed changed from how he remembered her. Her hair was longer, longer than in her profile picture. Miryam had great hair. He studied the lines on her face, pretty eyes he thought, brown like his, lovely arched eyebrows. He told himself not to stare at her breasts but somehow he knew Miryam had a beautiful bosom, when she stood he took in her belly & the way it sloped down to her groin, still all a mystery to him. Did she instinctively check him out in the same way? Romance was not on Miryam's mind, not then, he's probably gay anyway, she thought to herself. There was something mercurial about him, a shapeshifter, she found it difficult to even say how old he was.

Meanwhile Mina was thinking, If you don't mind me saying, that Miryam has a strong demon's body. Which for the record means, Miryam has a great body, strong & physical, "like mortal sin" – very sexy.

But back then, at that first time in the restaurant, Miryam was not alone. A chaperone, Mina thought. But not really, Miryam being Miryam, and seeing another woman dining alone, she started talking and dragged her onto her table. She's like that, always talks to people, makes friends. Her new friend, Elizabeth, gave Mina the once over, subtly, so she thought he wouldn't notice, but Mina, being Mina, he noticed. Did she know something he didn't.

So what did they talk about that night, everything and

anything, mostly the byeways of magick, their common ground. As the poet Peter Redgrove once put it, when people meet, they first have to navigate and negotiate each others' knowledge. So they three dined and drank a little. At the end of the night, Mina walked Miryam back to her B'nB and they said goodnight.

Next day at the conference, they did their own things but again in the evening, they met for dinner and shared a bottle of wine. Then the conference social, a grisly affair, upstairs in a local working men's club, whilst down below, paralytic locals threatened to punch each other. It was difficult to talk over the music. "I'm so drunk" Miryam yelled as they found a corner, swiftly followed by, slightly sheepish "are you married?" Mina hadn't removed his wedding ring though he always wore it on his right hand. "Well yes," he said, "I suppose I am". Miryam looked disappointed. Mina wondered what had brought that on now, the wine perhaps. "It's just" she went on, "it's almost my birthday, I haven't had sex for a while and well, I thought ... after all that stuff in your lecture about sexual magick, I wanted to celebrate my birthday with some. It's all sexual magick isn't it?"

Mina was silent, uncharacteristically not knowing what to say, and in a way, he'd already said it. It was not the entire truth, but he felt paralysed – the mechanics of the whole thing, just too complicated, they should have shared hotels or something. Somewhere in the back of his mind he felt sure a first night with a new lover needed something special –

surely not the back of a car or a shop doorway? It probably needed to be her guest house but how could that be. So he let the moment pass, there seemed no other way. And pass the moment did, Mina again walked Miryam back to her hotel, they hugged, but then separated and went their own way.

By the time Mina got back to his lodge overlooking the Somerset levels there was a message waiting for him on his phone.

"I am not sorry for being so direct, this is me being blatant. I might be drunk but I still have my limits. Don't let it affect our relationship. I will talk to you when I am sober. Good night."

Mina keyed a short, slightly awkward reply: "Not a problem, directness is good, you did good. But you win some, you lose some. For the best really, magical work often doesn't go with this kind of intimacy, though desire for companionship is a good human natural thing … and of course incredibly honoured and flattered, don't think me a complete ego maniac."

He lay in his bed thinking about what he had lost. He was a little depressed at the thought that their nascent friendship was probably over before it had really got anywhere. He went to the final day of the conference, hardly expecting Miryam to speak or remain friends.

But somehow they did …

The next day Miryam had left more messages on his phone. "Good morning. I was a bit drunk last night, but I'm very particular about the men in my life (sex or not) and when I like someone I will check boundaries. You know being Piscean...all good, and if anything, I respect you more."

To which Mina replied too quickly "Hopefully not too hungover? Wished I could have got drunk too, but I can't always cope with the aftermath. As I said, you did good, Very stimulatingly."

Emboldened, Miryam continued "I was thinking more about sex magic ..." which Mina interpreted as meaning, she was OK that they hadn't connected the night before, but that she was reframing things a little, maybe there was still hope.

Again, Mina keyed a quick, awkward reply

"Well yes, I'll keep that 'under the seal' as they say. Sex magic is a very unrequited thing in my opinion, not at all like normal intimacy. When you 'earth' the energy, ie actually have sex, seems to end the magick side of things. Or," Mina continued, "the sexual magic, I've been involved with, is a little known tradition called 'sahaja' (the spontaneous). There's a book called *The Hidden Moon*, it's all in there. It's complicated, as they say. It all has to be very secret and often doesn't involve conventional sex."

Miryam wondered if Mina was hinting he wanted a secret affair and messaged back

"Maybe we can have a cup of tea later?"

"Yes."

A First Dream Sending

(22nd February)

Mina returned to Oxford, Miryam stayed on before travelling to Brighton from where, she was to go to the airport and fly home. All the while their friendship grew in intensity, despite being conducted through internet chat, and social media. It often seemed to them they were just a breath away. They poured over each other's knowledge, obviously keen to keep the connection. Mina suggested Miryam buy what he thought might be a dream inducing tea made from the flowers of the Egyptian blue lily.

"I had the most wild and crazy dreams this weekend, I dream a lot."

"Tell me your wild dreams from the occult weekend if you like, don't hold back."

"OK, I need to process it all first. Lots of animal symbolism in strange hippie colours. There is this river or a water canal with some animals, bunnies? Or maybe beavers? They were swimming along in lines of three, in the water. Something gold, swans or geese."

Perhaps a little self consciously, Mina allowed the conversation to move into a more personal ground. "Very rich font of symbolism. I think Geb, he is a bit of a sexual athlete with his lady Nwt His emblem is a goose, so in Egypt they called him the 'old cackler'."

"I dream a lot and mainly in a symbolic abstract kind of way, which I have learned to understand and work with over the years. Dreams are the only type of divination (Oneiromancy) I can bother to work with."

"Saturday night was dreamy with the night air. Dreams can be a kind of theatre for magic ... perhaps the only one that really matters. There is a spells involving a donkey in the Egyptian Magical Papyri[2] that is supposed to send dreams to another person, sometimes even bad ones ... which they evil sleep."

"Never tried to send dreams before. I'm very good at lucid dreaming, and what some people might call journeying or astral traveling, which I can do when I sleep. I think it's my 'gift', I can do this kind of dream work since I was three or four years old."

"Now, that is the heart of the matter. I must admit I've only been successful in that kind of thing a couple of times. There is maybe some big difference between the Egyptians and us in terms of how we and they experienced dreams. To them it was always something you saw rather than something you did. The lucid thing, now that sounds like the same sort of skill as sending dreams."

"Then" said Miryam, "definitely I will give it a try. You

---

2 A collection of magical texts discovered in Egypt where they had remained hidden since their owner put them in a pot and buried them in the desert. Egypt had become Christian and things were difficult for the exponents of the old religion. The first modern publication by western scholars was under the title Papyri Graecae Magicae, or PGM for short. This title is misleading as it implies they were grimoires of Greek magick when in fact they are multilingual, and their context is totally Egyptian.

will have to give me guidelines on how to do this."

"Sounds like you already know how to do it, but we could try on the full moon, when it is like a mirror for the soul, at the full moon, send a dream."

"So the way I understand it is like this: on a full moon I decide what to dream, and who to send it to, and then go to sleep, and dream it?"

"Yes, perhaps some magical mechanics, something to incubate it, perhaps a snake or talismanic animal, I will try to sketch what worked for me."

"OK."

"Usually when I want to have a certain kind of a dream I have a simple method to induce it. Sometimes this means making a little talisman to start it off. I read in a book called *A Vision*, which is the spirit journal of the poet W B Yeats, how his spirits gave him this technique for evoking dreams:

'A symbol to be dipped in water after each night of sleep. Make a mantra over a small object, give it to her to wear without saying what it is used for. Charge with a simple clear image such as a flower...'

The dipping of the symbol in water comes in the morning, and is obviously meant to neutralise it. I had to look it up again, as I misremembered it, thinking one could actually use a flower petal as the talisman, which is a whole other, I'd say, equally valid technique. Fleshing this out, one would first breath the intent into it, then place it in water. Coincidentally some tantrik techniques use flower petals in a similar way.

One takes a petal, reminding oneself of what is in your heart, then breathe out, imagining the intent as landing on the petal, which one then drops over a statue. But getting back to Yeats and his wife Georgie's technique, I know from personal experience that it works.

A more complicated technique from way back, I did with my then on/off girlfriend, Amba. This is what we did. For several days previous she had been having bad dreams and felt that something or someone was sending malign thoughts her way. Because we weren't too sure who it might be, or even if it was really happening, that is all wasn't just paranoia, we decided to use a defensive intention, that would only be activated if there was something in the air coming our way. I think we wrote some words, maybe just 'evil go back', keeping it simple and leaving it to our deep minds to sort out what it was we really needed. It's then the basic sigil magick technique. We drew these words on her belly with eye-liner. I remember we also had a little glyph representing the mirror of Hathor, as a reflector. This was on my belly. So then, not to put too fine a point on it, if you don't mind me saying, but we had sex and forgot about the whole thing. It would have been the heat of our bodies, that dissolved the words and the sign, and our lust that sent it

off into that dreamy night air.

The next day we went to catch up with some friends, another couple, although maybe they were quite as well disposed toward us as we thought. When we met up with them they looked exhausted and, they said how they had just had a really terrible night! "

"About sending an evil sleep, do I send it to someone or just to the 'universe', the void or what? I don't understand really what I have to do."

"You mean the evil sleep thing, yes, quite aggressive magick, although whenever I did it is was defensive, only ever a case of 'evil on whoever wishes me evil'. Evil sleep is one of the more anti-social aspects of Egyptian magic. Evil sleep sent to a specific person or whoever happens to wish you or yours harm. It might help protect you and those beloved avatars of Seth?"

"I see, I don't really practice that kind of stuff myself. Usually I try to work with whatever energy, spirits or demons are within and around me to manipulate the outcome of things."

"Well then the other approach would be in trying to appear to others in dreams, there are no real issues there, as long as there is consent or a pressing need. It's said to be a difficult to bring off either way.

So let's go for appearing to each other in a dream, seems like a much more interesting, though difficult experiment. The intention is benign, just to make the connection, touch bases.

All this talk about dreams, I'm sure to have a vivid one tonight."

"Well I just might pop in your dream one night. Watch out for the animals you dream about, as I can appear in a few shapes!"

"I'm ready – hope so, it's very exciting."

"Let's see what will happen. I'll send you a dream on the full moon, the 3rd March, and if you want more, just say so."

Next day

"Miryam, did you start last night, I got something but maybe it was just anticipation?"

"What did you get? I might have been checking the lines of communication."

"I can't remember too much, but I know there was an elephant, and several notable encounters with a goat, who in my book, would be an avatar of the god Amun."

"A goat, that would be me. I love goats. I didn't think the elephant would cross the lines just yet, but if I think about it, the elephant is the one that opens doors and crushes all boundaries. According to my piscean logic, you seeing the elephant is like you answered the call on your side, does that make sense?"

"OK, that goat, Amun, he/she came several times over several dreams, and was feisty, perhaps angry about something?"

"Goats are feisty by nature. They are also cheeky and brave. I did not actively send any messages last night, just tried to see if you can see me or my avatars in your dream. The goat for me is related to the Baphomet energy."

"The spirit of the age. Definitely something in the air just now. The piscean age and the fish rising.

The elephant is very me too. The Indian thing, there's that, but I just learnt that they even have a small walk-on part in pre-historic, archaic Egypt, although you'll be sad to learn they got extinct by the time the pharaohs turned up."

"Well otherwise, that was a good start for very interesting dream work to come. I never had a partner for dream work. I could not find anyone that really understand dreaming and knows or is willing to experiment with the work."

"Me neither, but very much I want to explore. I have texts if you want more words, but maybe you have enough, they would be from my new writing project on 'Zar, visitations, memories', a territory into which we might cross?"

"Let's just experiment. I'll bring into this work myself and what I know (most of it is not written down, it's just mind techniques I seem to know how to operate). You bring what you know, and we play."

"Let's play."

"I'll try again tonight."

First love making

Then the strangest thing, Mina and Miryam made love in their shared dream. It was obviously in the air, but here's how it happened

"Mina, I had a weird experience just before falling asleep, maybe your dream is connected to that."

"Go on"

"Just before I fell asleep, in those few seconds in which we are no longer here but not quite there, I had this vision? visitation? not sure how to explain it. I could see, almost feel, a hand holding a glass with some sort of liquid in it to my mouth. I remember hearing something or someone asking me to drink from the glass. The odd thing is that I remember tilting my head so I could drink and drinking it, whatever it was. And boom it is morning. Very strange."

"The land which is at the gates of the dreamworld is even stranger than dreams."

"It did cross my mind that you might have something to do with that?"

"Not consciously, but it is something I do relate to and try to understand. It sounds just like one of those experiences known as 'the old hag'. You know? They are a bit like the 'evil sleep' we've been talking about from the Egyptian sources, by the sound of it. There is a way to stop them, a solution to break out of them so they won't recur."

Mina thinks to himself that maybe there is more but that Miryam doesn't want to say. So he describes his own dream instead.

"Last night I received a word of power, maybe it will help, something like Horeth, which is close to hiraith, which means 'spirit' in Welsh. But the word is also a fusion of Horus & Seth."

"I'm still thinking what my experience is all about. I might have to dream about it to understand it. Can you sort of understand the way I work? Do you think I need to banish something? Do you think that what I saw last night was somehow trying to stop our way of communicating, stop our experiment?"

"Not necessarily, it might be a demon trying to help us but getting overzealous. It's remarkable in its way. Last time I tried anything like this it was the sexy rite I mentioned before. And in case you're wondering, I am mostly celibate at the moment. This hasn't changed ... celibacy, for periods of time, it makes me more 'sensitive' when it comes to understanding dream work, it helps."

There was something he left unsaid. He was finding his dreams were full of sexual feelings for Miryam. In his dream she invited him into her bed and then to be inside her, he could almost feel the soft welcoming walls of her vagina embracing his penis as he went to her, and slid inside. Just wish fulfillment, he said to himself ... pushing the thoughts to the back of his mind, But what if she was feeling it too?"

Later

"You know Mina, sometimes, very rarely I meet a man, who will make me think, and feel, that I want to ground this psychic energy, into the basic practice of the wild dance of earthly powers. I just remembered one more thing from last night, I heard two distinct sounds. One sounded like the Hammond organ or electric piano. The other one was just white noise. And yes, I agree, celibacy intensifies the psychic power, but the wild dance of earth, it has its attraction ..."

So Miryam was feeling it too.

"But yes, I know and we discussed it before and everything is ok. I'm just being myself and open with you, if we want to establish good and deep dream work, maybe even a profound one, we need to synchronise our minds, in a very unique way. It's not very practical for us, all this earthly dance stuff, being 1000s of miles apart. But I just might pop in one night to take you dancing. Don't worry, we have lots to learn before that'll happen."

"I'll be your stud in the astral maybe? I like the thoughts of NakedTantra."

"Let's dance!"

"Next full moon is just after my birthday and just before yours. It feels perfect for some moondance Naked Tantra!"

* * *

As the new moon dawned, Mina posted an image of Meretseger from Cairo museum, the serpent deity that was venerated in ancient Egypt during the entire lunar month to come.

See image of Meretseger, Cairo museum,
at head of chapter

"This image! In the ayahuasca tradition she is the Queen of the Night. The queen of the jungle dreamscape, she is the

Great Teacher, Mother, Demon ... Lover. She always knows which face of hers you need to see."

"An unexpected connection."

"Most of my dream work skills come from her teaching. I see now the connection between the 'hand and the glass of liquid' experience from the dream the other night and the image above. They are very ayahuascaro symbols, I was actually thinking to send you this image in a dream, but it would have taken a lot of energy to deal with her; I didn't even try, but it seems to have happened spontaneously!"

"Oh! You better tell me again about the snake rite, it's obviously special."

"The Ayahuasca ceremony? There's a lot about it on YouTube. It is not a 'snake rite' as such or is it? One thing that almost all ayahuasca drinkers experience is the snake in all her aspects. For me it is like facing my greatest fears. I had a snake-phobia as a young girl and it took me years to overcome it."

"Well yes, I guess most of us don't feel comfortable with the snake."

"The best way to explain is via ayahuascan art, as the plant operates in our dream world. I have a feeling that when you see the art, which is based on people's visions, it would feel very familiar to you. First time I drank it, I felt like I'm coming back home, back to my dreamland."

Next day

"I just got an invite to an ayahuasca ceremony!

Mina, why are you obsessed with Seth?"

"Who says I am?"

"You want to make him a temple don't you, why and what would it be like?"

"Everyone has someone, a chosen deity, a projection of their inner self? Seth is there as my dialectical shadow, the flip side of the good god, of Osiris, or Jesus."

"So in a temple for Seth, what service would you offer? How do you see it?"

"It will not be a temple for Seth alone but the entire pantheon, the family of gods, which includes Seth, as it is, at the Osireion at Abydos. This is a place of mystery, where Osiris was killed and then resurrected, where his son Horus is conceived, the whole thing."

"What would we do? I don't usually ask for visions as I always get what I need. But I will try to see this temple. The lines of communication when in the ayahuasca ceremony are usually very strong, and I will try.

This is not going to be a NakedTantra stuff, I will probably ask for guidance. Let's both take a little of the blue lily so we can meet on the astral."

"I suppose it is also our tomb, and performance space, a place for offerings & a memento mori. There are pictures, Abydos was such a sacred place, a dream, not of recreating the whole, just the seed of it, or its core."

"Working with animals, I have understood my vocation is to help the dying animals to go through. It took me many years to accept this gloomy vocation and many hours of mentoring, for me, to see the beauty in death. My favourite type of burial is what I call 'raven's burial' where the dead animal is left in the field for the other animals to feed on. This is usually the smaller ones, cats, rabbits those kind. One cannot really leave a dead horse in the field, the stench would be too much! There's a tribe in Tibet which take their dead to a remote place on a mountain, skin them and leave everything, skins and flesh for the birds. I totally respect this practice."

"Natural death and burial, that would be a quintessential Sethian occupation. Like you, I think animals also have spirit, and can be our allies in the otherworld. In Egypt they called it the *akhw*. I have them and make offerings every new moon on the little shrine in the garden, for the departed animal friends and other immortals"

"What kind of offering? I need you to help me understand Seth, he is a complete mystery to me. I understand Isis and Osiris and the rest of them. I get Baphomet and Sophia, but Seth, I just don't know where or how to start. The only thing I get is the donkeys, and even that is not very clear."

"Offerings, just bread & beer, not so complex. Or smokey incense, and nightlights."

"That's a very nice offering, I will try to do that too. I'm not a very ritualistic person, so I'll probably forget. Something I have noticed the last few years is that each time I need to give an offering, I somehow end up bleeding, cutting[3] myself by mistake, or getting a nasty bite or a scratch from an animal, tree or plant. Took me a long while to see the connection, but now I just know when it's an offering type bleeding, and when it's not. Earth shamanism I call it."

"Well, no need for real blood, unless you have some. If blood is needed, then bit of red ochre in beer is fine as a substitute."

"OK."

"For a shrine just a simply 'trilithon', three stones, like the lintels of a gateway, just like the Hebrew Cheth (?). Those Hebrews in the Exodus story, Moses told them to make signs in blood to protect them from the angel of death, which seems to me a very Egyptian idea."

"Passover is soon, at the end of this month, Moses is the hero of that holiday. When blood is needed I just bleed a little, I'd never self harm or sacrifice anything."

"Passover figures in a lot of magic. The date coincided with Crowley's arrival in Cairo in 1904, and an opportune moment to restart his stalled 'Abramelin' ritual."

"People don't realise that there's a lot of magic practice in Jewish folklore. Take the protection from the evil eye, a very Middle Eastern practice, but also more advanced, as in kabbalistic magick. But it is sort of not talked about here, we are not supposed to practice magick. Think of the sacred vowels : YEHOVA = IAO and IAO = Seth, does it not? I'm

---

3   No self harming is implied.

a country girl, land and animals are my magic, when it comes to the intellectual kind of stuff, I need to dream it ... or feel it."

"IAO is the braying of donkeys, and at the same time a sacred formula."

"Donkeys cry four times a day, mornings, noontime, evening and midnight. And all the other times when they just feel like it ... (smiles). All the teaching I had so far about Seth, shall I call it Draconian magic?"

"Draconian, yes he's that too, ancient dragon, although the most common Typhonian interpretation I know, is from Kenneth Grant. Some Temples assimilate the "old dragon" with Seth?"

"Who is old dragon and remind me again why we are talking Seth?"

"Back in the mists of time, in the nameless aeon, people lived in fear of a monstrous serpent with the power of the evil eye ... its called different names in different climes, sometimes Leviathan, sometimes Tiamat and in Egypt, Apophis. She is the 'mother of all curses', male & female, like many fish, mercurial. Seth subdued Apophis with his own powerful eye, but in later times, the followers Osiris, merged both, into one evil god."

"In my 20s I was into Isis. I had two very powerful visions of her telling me all about myself, who I am, and where I came from. I was talking in tongues ... at the time I didn't know what to do with all that information, so I just didn't think about it. Later 'I found' The Fellowship of Isis, and joined. Isis always felt a little too big for me ... then I found Sophia, which I felt I can relate to more than to Isis.

Sophia, she's a bit of Isis isn't she? But then came Baphomet, which turned my world upside down, and inside out. It made me think that maybe I can have more than one deity? A woman can follow more than one idea, love, person or deity can't she? I remember you said something about Hathor, whereas Isis is the archetype of the ideal Egyptian woman, she is more about sex. Which made me think, maybe I should take Hathor as a deity?"

"Hathor is cool, a woman's equivalent of Seth in so many ways. Isis is very universal, a role model for women. I love her too. Hathor is definitely my kind of a deity, an older form of Isis, bless her, who is a bit of a chimera, her original overlaid by stuff borrowed from the others. Hathor, Holy Cow, that's her! The original beer monster, sex, drugs & rock n roll"

"Yep that's me. So, cowgirls that get the blues and big thumbs go for Hathor?"

"Big thumbs, Libido maybe ... the ...Clitoris ?... "

"You made me laugh out loud when I read this, seems like we both have a one track mind and Tom Robbins too! I don't know much about tantra and stuff but making me laugh like that from 2000 miles, away is very sexy. Now stop texting, go and dream about a big thumb."

Chapter 2
Baboons

"Doesn't matter so much about the size as long as it's hard" – After Rockbitch

(Mina remembered it as hard, Miryam, being Miryam, said "long & hard")

"He will make love to her with his heavenly fire. His will be as hard as steel when he enters her."
– *Myth of Seth & the Seed Goddess Hathor*

A First Naked Tantra Session
– Miryam's Initiation

"So, Seth got sick when he had sex with Hathor?"

"Hathor can be a bit much, even for lord Seth. An older form of Hathor is Bat whose name means female soul. I'd say the stream of thought we call tantra, it's all there in those old myths."

"I just wonder what Hathor did to Lord Seth ... mmm.. I start to get you now, and Seth.

Fancy some NakedTantra tonight?"

Mina texted a quick reply "Always."

"Bit naughty I know. But let's try."

"You have an Ayahuasca ceremony coming up soon?"

"Our ceremony is this Friday night, I'm really looking forward to it."

In order to invite Miryam into his dreams, Mina formed a firm intention that they would be together, then he held this idea in his mind before he went to bed, naked, hence the origin of "NakedTantra". To his surprise, it always seemed to work.

Next day

"Mina."

"Yes"

"There was something in the book *Tankhem* which I liked too. I'm going to look it up again:

"When you stroke me with a finger or tongue,
I quiver with excitement,

I love the feel of you, finger inside, tongue in me."
"When I stroke you with a finger or tongue,
You quiver with excitement
You love the feel of me,
Finger inside, your cock in my mouth."

Sounds familiar?"

"I didn't write that one did I? I forget, but I like to make people happy, which is why I channel these things."

"Yes, your words, but with a little variation of my own (smiles)."

"Yes, you made me very happy ."

"I will try to send you a dream."

"Lovely, hardon the size of ... Florida."

Try this:

'My tongue on your quiver,
Fingers separating lips
Wet with lust,
The dripping elixir of immortality."

"Hmmm, good morning Mina. You got me off guard, and now I cannot concentrate on what I was supposed to do ... Very good way to get in my head. I'm no poet, nor good with words really, but you make me want to try."

"Slowly, slowly, channelling the serpent goddess, kundalini-meretseger. Enjoy the buzz."

Later

"What a day! Couldn't stop grinning like a big fat Cheshire cat."

"Yes, a happy day but now I'm ready for sleep, long day tomorrow, catch up with you Friday I hope. I think these things have a beneficial effect on the aura, gives it sparkle, ... everyone notices, perhaps they even feels the attraction."

"Question time, Do you see any similarities between Seth and Ganesha?"

"Thoth and Ganesh? maybe on the basis that they are both born in an irregular way, they are both magical children. Thoth is born from Seth, Ganesh is born from Shiva. Both are male gods 'giving birth', so neither of them do normal stuff. Ganesh is said to be a god of the tantrik tradition, I would say Seth could also be one of those. Both are also about psychology, love or passion in contrast to other gods who sometimes just look like humans, such as a mother or a father, scaled up to the divine."

"I always thought of Seth as ground and boundary breaking, which made me think of Ganesh. I love Ganesh, he is the only deity that is always on my altar. If you could see what is going on in my mind now, you would blush. I had a dream last night in which my hair grew longer."

"A good omen according to the book,[1] it means 'something at which his face with brighten up' or as they say 'If you want to succeed, you have to succeed!' "

"I will."

"Goodnight"

Mina thought to himself, that one day, she's going to suck

---

1 *Supernatural Assault in Ancient Egypt*

my cock. Mina tried his best to ignore this thought for now.

Next day

"Miryam"

"Yes."

"I was just thinking, that all this we do is a 'good' way to stay celibate, and keep our mojo shining bright and strong. It is the alchemy of the demon lover."

"Funny you should say that, I bought a copy of *The Demon Lover* by Dion Fortune while in Glastonbury, and finished reading it just before I left England. Synchronicity?"

"Her books are full of Tantra."

"I have a few admirers at work, they are usually very shy and quiet. Since our session, two of them came out of their 'boxes' and made it very obvious they like me, poor bastards have no clue, and no chance…"

Now Mina said something he really didn't mean, but given the thousands of miles that separated them, he thought he had no right to say anything else. He inhaled and said:

"If they're attractive, then why not, take advantage of being hot?"

"Not my type, I'm very fussy with my men, take it as a compliment."

Mina exhaled

"You will have to tell me how to prepare for the practice, what would you do?"

"Matsyendra (Lord of fishes) is the Adiguru (primordial

master) of what is becoming our particular tradition, so what follows is, let's call it Piscean tantra. A shakti, ie you, aims to draw down the Yogini, She receives offerings, usually 'yoni puja' and in return she channels, in small bits, more of the tantra, which comes in the form of a dialogue between Shiva (Mina) & Shakti (Miryam). Can you manage all that?"

"Slowly in little steps."

"By the way, I'm sure you guessed that 'yoni puja' for yogini is cunnilingus, just in case that wasn't obvious?"

"I gathered."

"I never heard this kind of thing being done remotely as we are trying, we need to coordinate through time and location. Initially let's just focus on manifesting, seeing, the yogini. Let's just see if we can even connect. Is this the kind of thing you want to contemplate. How do you feel about this kind of work, the approach via imagination. Are you OK with it, it's a lot to take in?"

"I'm used to celibacy, when I feel I need something, I know what to do, or how to find someone I like. About a year ago, my old teacher sent me the *Tantra Magick* manual. I have read it, but I thought it was too much for me at the time, too much to really get into, without guidance, so I left it."

"None of this is in that particular book! The whole idea is to go beyond time zones and location, that's how I see it."

"Mina, I want you to initiate me, formally, you know, make me part of the Natha tradition. I feel ready, maybe it's a call? Everything is in synch. We can initiate a whole new thing."

"Initiation, yes consider it done, and already part of your future self. We will do it as the first part of ritual, but why not consider is available already! The sadhana I sent, seems rather a lot, but just seeing it, having it in mind, perhaps this is enough, helps us dream it for now. I've never done any of it this way before, its new territory, and difficult techniques, even in the real world. So we are treading on very experimental ground, attempting all, in astral steps."

"I know my way in the astral, I just need you to meet me there. Find a technique that will work for you, and let's play."

"Do you have a favourite rite to open things and protect sacred space? Something like Ritual of the Pentagram or whatever, if not, checkout the first section of *Tantra Magick* for an example. I use this pretty much as it is written, maybe with just a few mantras, to finish it off."

"Do you mean the opening rite: 'I salute the line of innumerable Naths…

I salute Shiva Shakti in my heart…' "

"Yes, that one from the Kaula cult, but whatever works, just thinking about precautions. Do we need an astral condom? I sense that you are pretty robust psychically, and don't get overwhelmed by voices off. Whereas. I admit, Pan gets to me sometimes."

"Yes I feel psychically robust. I don't get panic attacks. I learnt a lot on how to deal with the White Mage when it takes over. I feel ready for this. I've been looking for someone to experiment with this type of practice for ages. I think our minds are already connected in some strange tantra vibe.

I would like you to tell me in plain English, what would you like me/us to do after clearing the space, the opening rite and the mantras. Just be spontaneous and prepare to dream?"

"Yes. We will also see the moon for the first time this month. So if we draw it down into a cup or maybe just into ourselves. The moon and the yogini, let's just say they are one and the same. I think it might be. Somewhere in the back of my mind, I have a list of aspirations, well theoretically, priming, just things I'd like to happen, questions I'd ask, if ever I had someone who'd answer.'

The First Ritual (10th March)

Mina arranged a ritual space for the session, and, although the weather was mild, he lit the fire, to give the room an Indian style atmosphere.

He placed the yantra, a mystical diagramme that Miryam had drawn specially for that night, remembering the description of her doing it. 'I've put some music I like, and sat down, and then try sketching for a while, the one I like, and I wonder what can I do with it.' "

He played the track, *Cafe de Flore* by Doctor Rockit, it had already become one of their favourites. Miryam had played the same song when she made the yantra.

The finished image is very primal, like a voodoo veve, a sign, a sigil, emblem, magical shield or an Egyptian pictogramme, a universal symbol of the goddess, of Kali.

What else but the yoni, and two fish, Mina and Miryam, that seem about to plunge into its oceanic depths. Miryam knows they are making a new tantra

Assuming that all Yoginis are witches. The image is to act as an invite for one of the them to come, and to join their circle.

Mina, as the Hindus call it, is digambari, meaning naked, literally 'clothed in space'. The first time Mina had worked thus for a long time. Inner city life means lots of interruptions, 'demons' as he called them, intrusions. But there was something in the air, others around him had become noticeable more interested in what he was up to, what was going on in his head. All through the week he'd received little presents, all somehow connected with the work, all with a tantrik theme, for example the *kumkum*, a special makeup for tantric practice, a *mala* or ritual necklace, a new sarong. All this attention took him by surprise.

Miryam, was yet to become Miryam, that was to be the work for the first part of the ritual. They had discussed what name she should take when initiated, and eventually settled upon 'Miryam Devi'.

So, for the meditation itself, rather than creep self-consciously around the house, which he often found himself doing, he made a firm intention to do his thing. Therefore at the 'witching hour', perhaps a little before, he began the very intense practice.

First he danced around the temple space, naked and free, calling up the auspicious couples to guard the directions, and witness the rite. Then he saw Miryam, also naked, and he tentatively touched her body eight times, making the obligatory eight marks of tantrik initiation.

For her part, Miryam wrote a poem that best describes the night:

The Demon Lover

The music is on as I lie on the bed waiting.
I feel someone ask me to spread my legs open,
I can feel their breath on my thighs, on my yoni
My hands are guided over my body,
Like they are touching it for the first time.
This is not my usual sensation,
It's different, they don't feel like my hands....
I get up and dance,
I dance for awhile,
You dance with me,
I can see you.
I close my eyes
Was it you pushing me onto the bed
I feel your body against mine
I can feel your sweat
You touch me
It is all very, very sensual
I can feel your lingam pushing between my legs, searching,
I can feel your breath on my face,
You're inside me, we move together
One body. one breath.
I can't take it,
This is too much,
My body is shaking, sweating
Out of breath,
Heart pumping.
I offer myself to you!

"I didn't touch touch myself when all of the above was happening. My body reached an explosive orgasm, without me or anybody else physically, touching me.

Mina, as I lay in bed on my side, I could feel (your?) body next to mine, your lingam all hard. I never touched myself, but it felt like I was engaged in very sensual sex, love making, intercourse, whatever, with someone, it must have been you.

Leonard Cohen described it just perfect in those immortal lines:

> 'Remember when I move in you,
> and the Holy Dove she was moving too,
> and every breath we drew was
> Halleluja'…"

In his place, Mina was also making love to Miryam. He hadn't meant to, if anything he had floated the possibility of cunnilingus, yoni puja as the Hindus call it. But in his vivid visions, he was inside her almost immediately, she drew him to her. Pretty soon he made his offering, ejaculating his semen inside her. Their lust seemed never ending. Unlike Miryam, he could not swear he had not received some help from the 'hand of god', but, one thing he knew, it was as if he could physically feel the presence of Miryam's body.

Mina wrapped himself in his toga like clothes, and lay down again on his mat, he allowed himself to lapse into that uneasy sleep, a state between waking, and dreamless consciousness, that the ancient sages called yoga nidra, yogic sleep.

The yogini was still there, but now she was more relaxed, and was on all fours, so that her yoni, was presented to him. She's reminding me of our ancestry, the more primal side of us, a baboon or another ape, perhaps the banobo, all forms of the god Thoth. That name, the luscious syllables, rather than any other biological imperative. The yogini looks back over her shoulder at me. She knows how obsessed I am about this word. Ages ago I wrote a little erotic poem called:

> **Baboons**
> Sidling backwards
> On hand and knee
> Sex a flag
> Enough to make
> Arjuna
> change his gender
> Like baboons we tumble
> Biting nape's of neck
> Cock swollen like fire
> Your sex red
> Buttocks beautiful
> Nestle seductively
> In groin's crook
> Smooth skin strokes
> Fine hair where leg
> And abdomen meet
> Wriggling,
> My tip-tup finds a glide

Wet with moisture
Wet too with wanting
Teats that hand like dumplings
Lifted back
Nipple nestling gently
Tickling the palms of hands
My hand stroking you
Stroking you with my sex
Moving
Through the groove
Tickled
By mounds of hair
I am drawn inside
Twist and rich saliva flows
From mouth to mouth
Deeper we go
Reaching for the secret key
Fondling it lovingly
You grasp me within
My centre is in you
Bodies floating everywhere
Desire mounting
Upwards from within
Something bursting forth
Pulsations coming
Flesh with flesh
Fluids merging
Flesh without flesh
Fluids merging
Moments of pleasure
And we are again Baboons

Mina, so many things you wrote after that night are so intimate, like you knew me, like you were there with me, and not for the first time."

"That first session. I could feel you touching my lingam. Later, when I lay down, she, you, are still there, and we lay quietly together, hugging, our energy still streaming, chakras, especially the heart, connected. You whispered secrets in my ear, I can't remember much of them that isn't already expressed, but I feel sure, there will be reverberations over the coming days, in the penumbra, the afterglow."

Mina sleeps, thinking what a wonderful connection they have just made. There was something so convivial about it, all that baboon sex, the sexy beast before it all got so complicated. That love spoon, doesn't lend itself to oral sex, but one can do lots of other things, when she arches her back and thrusts her yoni, she obviously wants him to stroke her, the edge of my hand runs easily through the grove, she moving with obvious pleasure. When she becomes more firm set, steadying herself on a pillar, she wants me to thrust hard into her.

Later

"Oh Mina, The more you say it just become weirder and strange and so real. I left out some details from my story so we won't get it all mixed up. At one point, I had your lingam in my mouth just to see what you taste like, what you feel like. I could see you for a second, maybe I did see you. I've been practicing my astral travels for a very very long time. I never met someone that is so gifted and natural to this kind of practice. Never actually met anyone who thought it is possible."

"When shall we witches meet again? It takes a few days to recover. Part of me wants to do it all again, and another thinks, we probably should pace ourselves. You know how it is at the beginning of something, what do you think? A quiet weekend with just a little dream sex or more NakedTantra?"

"I so want to be baboons again, but I don't think I can do it just yet. I need some time to reflect, and to take it all in. You said yourself this was very unexpected. Karezza, caress then hold back, I once thought that this is what tantra is all about ... and couldn't relate to it. I never really understood the reasoning. Maybe it's me and my body, but I would rather die then hold onto an orgasm, and I would come anyway, so what is the point ... I know it sounds a bit dramatic, but I have been blessed with a body that knows what's good for it, and what it likes. Oral sex is great, I love it, but there is something very, very special, unique and magical when a lingam and a yoni unite together, becoming one, one ancient and mystical organ, bodiless. The force of life and death, definitely powerful."

"Karezza? No, I wasn't holding back, I came like you. But yes, let the energy build, and although noone wants to end too soon, sometimes coming quickly is inevitable given the intensity of it all, and strangely wonderful. I am a firm believer in letting go, seems healthier really, The post orgasmic mind works for me. When we initially spoke, I thought that tantra is mostly oral, but magick has just taught us something else."

"Don't hold back with your writing either, be as erotic as you want. I think my imagination is a bit different from most, I see things differently. What most people would see, I feel, and then I get flashes of sight, I don't really know how to explain it, I just hope you understand. Just remember that what you write, I can feel . . . We are going to have fun."

* * *

The next day Mina sent another poem

Tantra of Eternal Fornication
(I came so now you)
Yogini glances over her shoulder
Her yoni gaping & wet
Lips purple
Swollen With lust
Inside, wet walls expanding
I touch the key
They close, griping
And we are streaming,
Crinkles inside her
Ripples across a
member swollen,
ready to bust
They say
I came so now you
She says

She wants spunk to run out of her
To run down her leg
To be bursting with it
She wants to float
On me & in me
Back arched
Hips forward
Thrust deep into her
No movement
Quivers inside
Fondle me,
Suck me
Mouths
Covering each
Ka moving
From its base
Through wet urethra
Spurting now
In endlessly lusty
Gouts of shining
Sperm
From heart it streams
From secret channels
Never-ending
She can feel it
She can feel it
Inside
Two become one
One become nun
We are done

"Mina, thank you, so beautiful, my private demon lover. You asked me how I like sex, you inspired me to write this for you:"

Lover
I like it hot, sweaty and sticky
I like it cool, wet and fluid
I like it hard and fast
I like it soft and romantic
I like your fingers, lips, tongue and lingam
In my yoni
In my mouth
I want you to hug me
Kiss me
Fuck me
I want to feel your hands all over my body
My face
My hair
I want to sit on your face
Your lingam in my mouth
I lick you
Suck you
I'm going up and down
Slow and gentle
Hard and fast
I lick your root chakra
The tip of my tongue is at the edge of the void
I can feel you sweat, shake, holding your breath
You want to cry
You want to shout
You are going to come

But, no
Not yet
I'm not done
I kiss your inner thigh
I kiss your belly button
Light feather on your heart
I lick your neck
I bite your ears
We kiss
Tongues dancing
I sit on you and we ride
You can let go now
We are free
Two dark horses
Galloping into the sun

Meanwhile

In another time and place, two long distance lovers began exchanging erotic messages to ease the burden of separation. When collected together the messages make a short lover's story.

Lover's Story

I feel like it, now, too.

I'll sleep naked tonight and send you a dream.

I'll be erect much of it, no doubt.

So sleep naked. You'll be there. and I will too, and maybe, I'll keep my knickers On!

You know how much I like, want, to take them off. In the

dark I might have to feel you all over just to check if you're really nude.

I like the way you inspect my body. The feel of your hands on my breasts, on my fanny, squeezing my bum.

Snuggling behind you, cupping your breasts, then rubbing your belly. Kissing the back of your neck as I feel you. Then *down there*. If my hand slips inside your knickers, and feels your fanny, will you be wet?

I missed you, of course I'm wet when you touch me!

Opening the little wet clam, feeling just inside. Your clit is hard, my fingers slide over it, play with it. I'm wanking you with my fingers. The hood moves back and forth.

My body is shivering and quivering, I can't stop it. Maybe you lick it too?

OK, I'll lick you now, finger inside, as I lick and suck your clit. My cock is so hard, might have to push it in soon, as I wank you.

I love the things you do with your tongue.

I lick more, tongue inside, cock wants to go in there soon, but you've got to really want it.

I think I'll come now, don't stop licking me, put your finger inside!

I'm finger fucking you, whooshing around, then deep, then out, and in deep. All the time licking you off.

Delightful waves of pleasure.

I can feel them.

That's so good. I'm going to explode. It's time to push your cock in. Yes, push it in. I want to feel you inside me. Push it in now!

I thought you'd never ask! Pushing through the silky wetness inside you. Resting in you, all hard. Just breathing and pushing. My weight on you.

Heaven! I can feel you deep inside of me. Stay inside. We must carry on from this in the dream tonight.

So inside you. All this again in our dream.

Chapter 3
Fire and Water

"Rise up nimbly and go on your strange journey to the ocean of meanings." ...Rumi

So after that climax what is next to do but a cool headed evaluation.

"we have to keep a level head and..."

"yeah, right..."

So a week later, still in March, they were both still disentangling the threads and tripping on the fumes. For Mina, the earthing of their magick, manifesting as poetry and creativity was the name of the game really. At the risk of boring his Miryam, he recommended to her, the work of the famous poet William Butler Yeats, who had, after a long fallow period, suddenly found earthly love, but also a contact with those inner spirits he had longed to meet in his many years of occult study. Yeats knew a lot of things, and when his new lover began channeling what sounded like ancestral voices, his first instinct was to bring his accumulated book learning to bear, to analyse and codify. But soon enough, the spirits admonished him, disabusing him as being too solar, the familiar, and unsuccessful pattern of his life up to that point. The purpose of the messages was a different kind of magick, and of gnosis. If they were offering anything, it would be only 'metaphors for poetry'.

So, they both agree, they needed to keep a level head, and not get too carried away, remembering what they thought of as their *Piscean* traits, which in this instance meant a capacity for craziness. Sex, is, afterall, a very intoxicating thing, even though from some standpoints one might not consider what they had done, actual sex, but somehow, they both just knew things differently. They were changed by what they had accidentally invoked. It now felt that they were real lovers, though they hadn't completely admitted it, they were projecting their feelings into the personas they had created, which had now taken them over. It was Mina and Miryam who were falling in love, or remembering an ancient romance, and not the x and y who had created those personas in the first place. In a phrase often on Mina's lips, it feels like we are eternally fornicating.

"Mina, you can call me any name you want and like, but at the end of the road it is me, and we are you, so I just say it as I see it. But the name Miryam is good too, it has been in my family for generations."

Mina was good with words, well, so they both were. It's another Piscean trait, this capacity to glamour, to mesmerize others and each other, with the power of words.

"Just saying, we better remember that now and again."

"Your capacity to glamour with the power of words is huge and vast, but I have my own ways to glamour you."

"Do you understand the depths of the ocean we are diving into? Because I don't. But the waters are of fine colours, of emerald and turquoise and light blue. I can see through it and it's very deep."

Mina felt sure that what they did fall into, was the hinterland between India and Old Egypt, he even called it Indo-Egyptian tantra. It was old but also new. In India there is a style of esotericism known as 'Sahaja', meaning 'the spontaneous'. It cuts across the normal boundaries and is thus sometimes said to be antisocial, if only for the reason of its secrecy, and ability to cause upset when those secret connections are revealed.

Mina had been exploring this mystery for several years alone, mostly in his own head, and with some success. He'd written about it, and people had found things of value in what he had discovered. But now the current had delivered him to

Miryam, and she to him, and from now on they were to explore together as partners, empowering each other. Hence Miryam was 'shakti' meaning female power and Mina 'shakta', the male counterpart.

Miryam replied "You tell a very good and magical story, I like to dream your stories. As long as you keep your stories coming, I will dream them to life."

Egypt's so-called 'demon' god Seth, had always held a special place in Mina's heart. He felt that all of the ideas they were now exploring, all the things above, were also somehow implicit to the myths of this god. For instance, his myths were always so sexually charged, the secret thread that ran through so many ancient magical books. The 'secret'.

They both felt blessed to have found a natural connection that was, at the moment, working so strongly. They knew they would channel more secrets to do with the dream and imaginal realm, with healing, psychology, music, dance, shamanism, ... gnosis. Much of this they would share, some immediately, some later but for the time being, they would not reveal each other's full identity. They were now always Mina and Miryam, Miryam and Mina.

"I once knew a Soror Tanith, now long dead but not completely forgotten. She was always very proud of her ability to channel 'Libers', which is what the magi call their most special channelled books or is it 'Sefer'? Will we do the same?" Mina was excited

Miryam thought to herself, how a good deal of this is all

so tangled up in the sheer joy of union, and, sexual fun. And what would be wrong with that.

"Yes, of course, replied Mina, reading her thoughts "inevitably so, although we can dream, be a bit preposterous, keep our eyes on the, possible, prizes, and in the meantime, create more poems, art, and dialogues between the gods. And while we are at it, we could be recreating, for ourselves, all the ancient pagan techniques of magick."

"PS. just in case I'm getting too carried away, here's today's sexual fantasy, when we do meet, in the real life, I'd like to share a nice hot bed, naked, but strictly no sex, apart maybe from embracing. It would be a long night tantrik dream, do you think we'd manage it?"

"yeah, right ... & No, I don't think we could manage it."

Liber MMM

"Mina."

"Yes"

"Something very strange came up this afternoon, not sure what it was, but it was a message from Aleister Crowley. I don't know much about him, only the usual gossip, and his famous Thoth Tarot deck, I think the message was for you! I'm not sure if you are aware of that, I think we are writing a new Liber MMM? Both of us Morgan, Mina, Lord of the Fishes and I Miryam, MMM."

"Mysteria, Mystica, Maxima".

"What is that?"

"It is the name for an organisation within an old magical Order. One of the magical Orders Aleister Crowley, founded which has another funny name or rather acronym, which is Argentum Astrum, which, one way or another means *Silver Star*. But then it crops up in one of his sacred instructional texts, yet another acronym, HHH. Occultists do like to cloak things in this kind of luscious language. In other words, it's pointing us to one of Crowley's magical books, or what he thought of as his sacred texts, certainly one full of instructions."

"So, it is an important text?"

"Well, yes, I suppose so, it concerns one of those great quests of the adept, the raising of the fire-snake Kundalini. I have to admit, there's something about the language of this text that I couldn't really relate to when I first read it, but maybe I, we, should look again. Lots of serpents in there, sometimes they bite and sometimes they dance, like two snakes mating, though Crowley did not quite say it that way. Does he mean for us to complete the circle? Try to remember more of your vision? Do you fancy more magick?"

"Tonight, I would love to lie next to you in bed, body to body, relaxed, embracing, kissing, dreaming The Road To Nowhere …

The higher the frequency, the busier it gets. Everyone wants to go higher, channel higher information, higher realms, higher entities, higher frequencies. There's hardly any room left for us to fly anymore. But why fly if we both can swim and dive?

We can go for the deeper frequencies, The place where most have to hold their breath and panic, but we have gills, we can go as deep as we like. The snake Yemanja will guide and protect us. The magic is old and comes from the oceans. The oceans are the old sky full of new stars."

"Deep stuff, the oceanic feeling. Start again from the beginning and tell me more about what Crowley said?"

"Aleister Crowley, he is not a person I would normally think about, not even for this magick that we do. I tried in the past to read some of his stuff but couldn't get my head around it too dramatic and theatrical for a cowgirl like Miryam ... I think I was telling my friend about the rite, our trance-astralic experiment ...he said, I was glowing when I told him my story, and then, I just thought of Aleister Crowley, he crept into my mind just like that, but somehow I knew that this is something to do with you. I don't know enough to make any sense of him appearing to me, so I assumed, it's to do with you, being a cunning Mina Nath, and all that ... but on second thoughts, Liber MMM, it is meant for both of us ... I think at the end of all this, when we come to this point again, a big mystery will be solved.... MMM."

Later

"Mina, my Love."

"Yes."

"Do you remember that day we sat at the coffee shop and I told you I want you? You didn't know what to say for a second, so you came with the question, if I want a relationship

(I knew that inside your head you were saying yes, I want you too, but you thought to yourself, this woman is so intense … I don't know what to do.)

So I said; no, how can we? I'm here and you are there. And I said, I don't think we could have a relationship like normal people do, it won't last, we will forget to eat, work, breathe and will end up in a loop of mad piscean dimensions. Not healthy at all. I'm not very good with the domestic stuff, being a piscean woman, I never had to worry about all that stuff, my partners usually took care of me, so I could just be me. Sound familiar?

I don't want to upset your lifestyle because I don't think I can give you any better alternative. I live a life of a cowgirl, most men find it hard to cope."

"Babalon?"

"Babalon, let me tell you about Babalon, I was just looking at my diary from a while back, fire and water, that's her, like Oshun, Orisha of the rivers and sweet waters. Here's how she found me. I'd been invited to take part in a ceremony of a different tribe, they share the same path of the Serpent and the Panther, but the practice is different. My tribe like to dive into the pool of the void, through its darkest tunnels and halls until it turns into light.

The other tribe practice the way in great light and celebration, even at the darkest moments somehow they find a way to celebrate with a beautiful practice.

I thought that it is the perfect space to evoke Babalon. I

needed to get some answers from her, so I put on my red dress and made a little tobacco offering to the fire. Then I waited for her to give me a sign; when it comes it is like the rhythm of the ayahuasca dream state of mind:

> The serpent is awake,
> Is coiling in my tummy and heart,
> It is moving and winding, its scales are bright red,
> It is getting ready to move up toward my neck,
> I'm terrified it is going to swallow me,
> It changes into a serpent-like flower,
> Changing its colour from red to yellow,
> More and more serpent-like flowers are popping around me.
> I can hear the Oshun song from the distance,
> I am singing it,
> I can hear Babalon whispering in my ears,
> To understand me, go with Oshun.

I get it...

At first the Scarlet Lady and Oshun looks like they have nothing in common. Oshun is the Yellow Lady of the rivers ... but to embody the will and the passion to create magic and change, you need to move in a wavelike motion, to be fluid like water.

Babalon rides the flames of the ever-burning fire. If you look closely at the flames, you can see that they have a strange fluidity. Fire, like water, always has to move, to expand, never standing still. So both ladies share the same qualities. Oshun, the watery aspect of Babalon, Babalon the fiery aspect of

Oshun. You cannot create magic from still water that lacks fluidity.

You cannot create magic from still and tamed fire, which will soon burn out and die.

In the morning after the ceremony closed, I stood by the fire talking to the shaman, when something caught my eye. At the side of the fire was a statue of Shiva holding the Trishula[1] trident, and next to it two further Trishula, made from iron. I couldn't believe my eyes. I'd dreamt of those very Trishula the month before!

When I asked the shaman what he uses them for, he said what I have always known: at the ceremony the Trishula helps destroy the three worlds that we find so hard to let go of. After the ceremony, we arrived at the here and now, with joy, beauty and bliss in our hearts. Who said that dreams can't come true??

Om Namaha Shivaya
Viva Oshun
Hail Babalon."

* * *

---

1 Lord Shiva's trishula is supposed to destroy – the physical world – attachment to gross, the illusionary world which seems so real; the world of the mind – the ahamkaar or ego which is a barrier between Me and HIM – thus transforming the devotee to be in the third world that is the world of spirituality, leading to oneness with Lord Shiva, a single non-dual plane of existence, that is bliss alone (Wiki)

Somewhere, in the back of Mina's mind he remembered hearing a warning, especially for the male magician, a warning of the tempting, intoxicating promise of an earthly Babalon. The woman with quivering hips, who in tantra, turns one's world upside down. He let the thought pass.

"Mina, the chemistry between us is unique, strong, sexy and powerful. I could see it straight away, and knew we could have something, didn't know what then, but know for sure now. I want you as my magickal partner, my astral lover, we can dream together and create a new path for us, that maybe one day, others will follow."

"How could I refuse."

"I still want to fuck your brains out, and I will, But we can do it only when we meet and who knows when that's going to happen? Maybe in the summer, next month is too soon, I told you why already. We are onto something good and wonderful, can you see it?"

"I see it, it terrifies me, but I see it."

"Do you want to stop it before it even begun?"

"Of course not!"

The Ritual

(In the near dark moon towards the end of March)

27th Lunar day – sacred to yogini Balaka

"Mina?"

"Yes."

"I've been getting more strange messages from Aleister

Crowley all day, now it's getting late, we need to coordinate our timelines. We meet at the witching hour, do you think he will barge in, will he come?"

"He might, are you OK with that?"

"I'll live."

In Miryam's time zone it would actually be more like 2am when she starts her opening rite. Now the ritual is more complex, Miryam, whose love of music is immense, has created a special playlist to act as the ground to their rite. In their first work they had also used musick, though more randomly chosen; Mina listened to ambient sounds from a radio station, Miryam to one of her uploaded soundtracks. This time they shared the same specially prepared playlist.

Miryam burns the incense blended for the Sea Priestess, she's never done this before, she finds it very heady, but gentle, thinking it should creep up on them through the limbic system and hit the old brain, the seat of the Dragon. She hopes that in his temple space, thousands of miles to the west, Mina is lighting the same incense. The Dragon is awake!

As he begins, Mina wonders whether they will match the frisson they felt during that first breakthrough meditation. What drives him on now, he realises, is a clear longing for Miryam's body. It's off the scale, quite different from how they were when they first met in Glastonbury. Perhaps it is always this way, their practice has become one that amplifies lust, and then, using this as the mechanism, they travel and they dream. Mina's sexual fantasies are out of control. He forgets to listen to what the inspired shakti, Miryam, is saying. "I am so enjoying the moment of union" he says to himself, wondering, will this be enough? Enough for what, enough to do the work.

Mina cannot settle, cannot still the internal dialogue, the ideas floating up to the surface, like bubbles in a liquid. Why this great outpouring of words, the earthing, the manifesting perhaps. "You cannot tell a story until you know how it will end and for that you need an end ... and we haven't got there yet – perhaps we won't ever." Question "can anyone live the way we dream?" She says "no, but did you ever know you could dream like this? It will help people to dream."

"Yes, Mina agrees, we are churning the ocean of milk alright, out of which comes the elixir of immortality but also ... sometimes ... poison."

The new Kali Yantra is on the altar, the one Miryam has drawn with the two fish about to enter the oceanic depths of the goddess ... again.

A few minutes to midnight, the Sea Priestess playlist sounds through their room. They make the invocation.

For Miryam, the hour is indeed late, she is very tired, and not a little stoned. She lies on her bed before diving into the mirrored pool. She calls out to Mina, thinking to herself, this time I want to see you, not just feel you; everything is to be even more real. So she dives deeper, just a little more than last time.

"I can't wait to see you" she thinking to herself. Then a

thought crosses her mind, "I'll come and get you. I'll just come to your umbra zonule!"

All day Mina's mind was leaping ahead to the evening session together. As the midnight hour approached he took his dragon seat and opened the umbra zonule as agreed, skyclad. He listened to the E de noite chant several times, as planned.

Canto De Nana
E de noite e
De noite ate de manha
Ouvi canta pra Nana

It is night and
it is night until dawn
I hear the chant for Nana

He remembered what Miryam had told him about Nana, the 'grandmother' goddess, the old one ... There was a happy memory attached to that chant, in the message, Miryam had written: "I'm going to smoke a little and go to the shower, will you come with me? Tell me what would you do ?"

The music ended and was replaced by ambience. Spine upright, he was waiting for Miryam to come to him. Then a distinct sensation of someone there. Mina's lingam becomes erect. Delicious waves of arousal waft over his body, between meditation and nidra, as the Hindus call yogic sleep. He feels a cool breeze on his skin, as if someone was blowing on his erect lingam.

In an instant Miryam is in Mina's temple. Now he sees her, and in a flash he is flying towards her, his arms wide and inviting. They kiss and kiss and kiss. It's all very fast and intense.

"There are lights all around and through us and coming out of us. I can feel your hands over my body, like you are making sure it is me, that I am real. I am! I'm right here with you! When you kiss me it is like a thousand suns exploding in my head. You're on top of me, the old fashion way. I like it, I like to feel the weight of your body on my body. We're moving fast, very fast. You kiss me again. There's something very bright in your eyes. I kiss you and before I know it, I am drifting away.

Mina is in Miryam's room, she is asleep in her bed, or apparently so. He folds back the sheet and gets in beside her. She is warm and convivial, sleepy but welcoming. We're like virgins to each other, as if we've never done any of this before. His hands intuitively goes to her breast, her nipples are erect, "I fondle and kiss them, gently squeezing."

He wonders if Miryam is wet... down there. As if reading his thoughts, she allows her knees, to fall aside onto him in the bed. Her thighs are wide open, like a dancer, inviting him to feel her there. She is indeed very wet, glistening and receptive. He slides a finger into her, and she meanwhile has found him and is slowly stroking. All the while they are kissing.

Mina remembers the work. Miryam wants him sitting upright so she arranges herself over him, his member inside her. They are in a moment as deeply inside each other as they could be. Her labia, her yoni, purple and pressed against every part of him. An embrace, like a perfect opening or door. Mina reaches and fondles her buttocks, separating the cheeks, a crupper, like a small horse, supporting them. They hug, supporting each other, kissing and sharing breath. Their heart chakras connected. After years of searching, Mina has finally found his heavenly mare.

Later

In the morning Miryam sent another message to Mina, telling him what she had experienced.

"All I remember from that point, is me drifting away, sometimes swimming, sometimes flying. Each time I came round you were inside me, touching me, kissing me. I must have woken up at 7am that morning (forgot to turn the bloody alarm clock off) and you were there, in my bed, real, spooning me, cupping my breasts in your hands ... I had to go to the bathroom and realised I was bleeding ... I have charged our sigil."

"With menstrual blood?"

"Yes ... I got back into bed, put my arms around you, kissed your back and went back to sleep ... I woke up again at 10:30. You were gone, but I'm all wet and sticky like you just been in me, here."

"To see you like that, was so real. I had to go into a very,

very deep trance, deeper than I usually would (and I like to go deep.) Once you had me in your arms, I felt safe, I could let go and dive into the depths of the mirror pool of secrets."

Mina replies

"We were connected, and stayed so for a long time. When you sensed I was sinking, you brought me back with your yoni, floating in a dreamy, almost orgasmic state. We stayed this way for a very long time, all the while you whispered secrets to me, head on my shoulder. None I can remember, but they will emerge slowly, of this I am sure.

Where did the time go, I stopped, not from tiredness, the fire had died down and my candles were finished. Before I left, Shakti lets me come inside her, (she says in the old fashioned way). I push inside her, again and again. On my seat, is a great gooey wet patch, has Miryam been, her own juices flowing down. And of blood, reminds me of this poem I'm sending you now."

How the Fisher King was wounded
In one life,
I thought of nothing but,
How hard my cock was,
And how many times.
You, Morgan LeFay
You were there too,
As am I,
As we always are.
Again I am magician,
Who thinks,

the secrets of,
Of Immortality.
Androgynous woman,
Who acts like a warrior,
Who wears a man's kilt,
Tied with a woman's sash.

You,
in a rage,
finding me with another,
Fling your burning spear at me,
Aiming for my groin.
But thinking better of it,
Shift slightly,
And pierce my thigh,
Till the blood runs down to my Shins.

I can still feel the sting,
And the pain that left,
Me puking & sinking.

Now you say,
Why are you so grey,
Your eyes so dimmed,
Whilst my hair is good,
Lustrous,
Falling down to my sexy breasts.

H H Hard Liber,
The finale,
Fuck my own brain,

Didn't work for me.
We knew long ago,
Better do that to another,
Gently fuck each other's brains out,
In a dream if need be,
For whoever says liberation,
Is a solitary thing,
That cannot be had in the arms,
Of a lover,
We shall prove them wrong.

Lover's Story

"Come to bed."

"I'd love to. You all naked?"

"I have a T-shirt and knickers on."

"Sounds a bit restrictive round the fanny, might want the air."

"So help me take them off."

"Let me take mine off first, so I can rise free and check you out a bit first, feel you through the fabric of your clothes."

"Help me take my shirt off, It's a bit tight."

"Your nipples are erect, I have to feel them first, then I'll pull it off. you have such lovely breasts."

"Take my nipples in your mouth."

"I'm sucking them, they feel so good. My hand strokes your bum, then your pussy through your knickers, under the cloth."

"Kiss me!"

"I'm kissing you, hard, my tongue in your mouth, yours in mine."

"I missed your kiss Mina, kiss me for a little more."

"I'll kiss you and kiss you ... I won't stop, might even come from kissing you, sucking your saliva, so sweet."

"Can you feel my heart?"

"Yes, beating fast like mine, we sharing breath. Our hearts merge as we keep kissing, the breath of life."

"One rhythm."

"Yes, somehow we breathe into each other."

"Yes"

"Companions of Seth, sharing breath, conspirators – orgasmic really."

"Your breath circulating in me I can feel you inside and you can feel me."

"You can kiss my neck now maybe behind the ears."

"You'll have to get very close so we are hugging each other. Knickers quickly off? But very close and emotional –"

"Now upright, legs arranged over each. I have missed you too."

"Hugging you with my legs, pulling you close to me."

"So much love I want to give you."

"So give, Kiss me."

"My cock is against your fanny as I kiss your neck. Doesn't have to go inside but your labia are kissing me down there too. The lips spread, shall I touch you?"

"I can feel your cock hard and ready. Touch me."

"Still kissing you. I reach between your legs and feel the wet groove, from bottom to clit in continuous delightful strokes."

"I love the touch of your fingers."

"Feeling your clit now, exploring your secrets. Moving the hood, gently stroking. So wet now."

"Mmm I like it!"

"A finger or a cock inside?"

"I want your cock inside me. But go in very slowly."

"So we can breathe together."

"I lift your bum up, separateing the cheeks and then you lower slowly onto me, you sigh as we join. Almost coming, both, but just hovering there."

"Ahhhhmm."

"When joining together, our hearts miss a beat. Inside, your vagina caresses me, I can still feel your clit caressing me, so lovingly, we are merging."

"I can feel you inside me, you fit perfectly."

"Rocking back and forth to the rhythm of our hearts, our breath, our bodies. Wonderful sensations inside and through the whole body, your vagina pulsing. We should stay like this, floating into sleep together."

"Yes."

"Connected from Crown with a kiss and Malkut with lingam/yoni."

"Best way to go to dream."

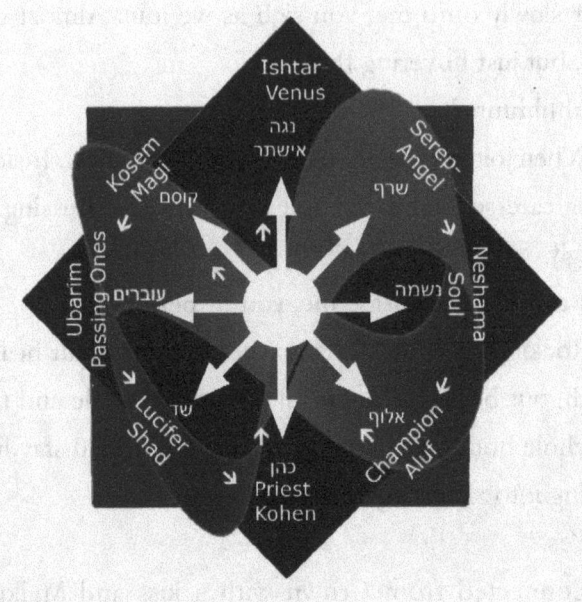

Chapter 4
The Kiss of Life

> Happy is the moment, When we sit together, With two forms, two faces, yet one soul. You and I
>
> — Rumi

Fire and water

Fire and Water, Miryam and Mina. Miryam, she's a fiery mare, the one I've been looking for all these years. Babalon or mare fire, it's another really old name from India, not so well known in our circle, but pretty much synonymous with *kundalini*, the goddess and fire serpent.

"Mina, I have no words or name for what it is that is happening, but somehow everything is falling into place, dreams and information I received in the last few years, have started to unfold in a very unique and new way. How did you find that door? I thought it was so well guarded and tucked away."

"I love that you say that, this thought, that I found a special door, it makes me feel very special too. And we're going to meet again ... in the flesh. Looking back over the record, I have to keep reminding myself, ourself, that all these experiments so far have been in the dreamtime, in virtual reality, in the imaginarium. Back at the beginning, we called it a magical experiment, but now it has made this unstoppable urge to do it over, but for real, in real time.

I confess its making me a little anxious, maybe you too, or maybe it is just me. I bet you think this is a strange attitude to get from a man, we're not supposed to be like that, self-doubt can be self=defeating, makes us look weak, so even though we may feel it, we're not supposed to admit it. It's not attractive, not commanding. but sometimes, your unbreakable certainty that we can replicate the kind of ecstatic magical union we've enjoyed, but in reality, as we have in our imaginal world, I confess, I do wonder whether, or how it will be. Well you knew already, that I am a very lunar man, that is what I bring to the equation. So for now, I'm basking in your solar fire. So yes, I've made all the plans for the meeting at the summer solstice as we agreed, don't worry about that, I'll be there, although that is still two months away, and a lot can happen in the time."

Demons

"We can't write our story without knowing the end, well I don't see the end yet, and maybe I don't see it at all. I understand about the poisons that surface but a poison for one, is a medicine for another. Remember, light and dark, yin and yang, black and white etc. We plunged into that mirror pool, and there are so many reflections of things to be, and all the possibilities they can be manifested. We only have to choose, would you take the apple?

So just make it as it is; an *experiment*, two people, two countries, one mind, experimenting in tantra meta-magick, cosmic astral travel to the land of no boundaries, looking for the doors of perception.

If we are ever to write our book, we will awaken two ancient souls into the here and now, so we need to tread carefully. And if we ever do it, this will open a door for a new experiment. People everywhere are turning to virtual reality games, to escape and dream. But they forgot how to dream. But what if they can use their minds like we do, and what if they really can join the lucid dream reality? Then it will be a very strange world indeed.

The Dragon Seat which you say you have in your Umbra Zonule, a place, a seat on which to meditate and to dream. My Dragon Seat is tucked away deep in the back of the ancient brain, the reptilian brain, the place where memories and dreams are born. I sit there and wait. Now the Dragon is awake.

And yes, I say, you are worrying too much about what will happen when we will meet again. I think you should stop, we have something very special, and it is real. I have a feeling you don't fully understand, what I mean when I say it is real, but you will, in time, soon hopefully. When we meet, I wish it could be now, we'll do what we can, it will be fast or slow, long or short, hard or soft, whatever, it will be wonderful, and just the way it is supposed to happen. We can always dream, and when dreaming, we are so close to each other, how can it not be wonderful?"

I'm thinking of how we can meet around the Solstice, in Glastonbury. We will need a place were we can do what we like with no interference, some food and wine, and maybe some blue lily too.

Then we can practice lucid dreaming reality or to say it simply, I will shag your brains out!

And one last thing. Did I tell you Miryam is a healing name for me? I feel that taking this name on is part of my role in changing the karma for the women in my family. So many Miryams with hard and bitter, sometimes really bad lives. I knew I had to take this name, and once you added the Devi to it, it felt just right and I just knew the healing had begun, Thank you."

Abramelin

"Miryam?"

"Yes, I'm here."

"I'm walkabout, if you are in your bed we can exchange sexy words now, I have a new scenario for you, to help stimulate the mare-fire, when the time's right. But just out of interest, in real life, what sort of bed do you prefer, a futon on the floor, or a traditional bedstead with a mattress?"

"I stopped using futons sometimes in the 90s. but I know what you're thinking. So if you to kneel beside it, you can do whatever you like ..."

Later

"What celibacy means to me, is not touching myself.

The magic we found, that we do, is, that I can orgasm without touching myself, without you touching me."

"Wanking is such fun though. Especially with someone else involved to get you going. I am not trying to get you going, honest. But wanking with me inside you, that's a thing, one of the many lovely things. It was quite a sex session last night, can I really fill you up, you are the great ocean afteral?"

"You do, and you will. Tell me about the Abramelin ritual, I just saw the name but don't know what it is."

"Abramelin is a special magical rite that begins at Christian Easter, or Jewish Passover, if you prefer."

"The Hebrew calendar is a lunar one. Passover is celebrated each year in the month of Nisan when the moon is full, which sometimes falls on the end of March and at other times in April."

"As you can probably guess from its title, the Abramelin is the work of a medieval Jewish magician, Abraham of Worms. Georg Dehn is the author of the most complete edition. I exchanged a few letters with him. He told me all about his adventures in Egypt trying to find some of the places mentioned in the book. The whole thing starts off like a adventure novel, which is maybe the best way to see it. I think we agree the novel or a romance is a pretty good way of presenting magick. There's some sort of overlap between the whole business of story telling and magical work. Gurdjieff's *Meetings with Remarkable Men* does a similar thing for me."

So, the Abramelin story claims to be this guy Abraham's account of his quest for secret knowledge, which, he eventually finds, in Egypt. In the book he ascribes his success in life, spiritually, materially and financially to its secrets. The book is also his last will and testament, where he tells everyone how he wants his property to be divided. His knowledge of the mysteries of Kabbalah goes to his oldest son. The mysteries of magick, which is sees as a different thing entirely, he leaves to his youngest son Lamech, for whom the book was written. To his daughters he leaves money, and a decent amount at that. Some doubt whether this is authentic Jewish culture, would a Jew really name their child Lamech, what do you think? It finishes with an account of how to invoke an angel via a very long magical retreat, and then a whole series of talismans, all in the form of magick squares."

"Lemech is a very old fashioned name, which I'm not sure if it was ever one real people used. If you called someone a 'Lemech' they would be clumsy and confused, a fool. But on the other hand, Lemech is Melech spelt backwards and Melech = King. So I think that every time you come across this name Lemech you have to read more into it between the lines. The only time I ever came across this name, is in some old Jewish folklore, the Lemech character is always something like the Tarot Atu the Fool."

"And the Fool is the most interesting of tarot cards, the whole sequence that follows is sometimes called 'the fool's journey' from fool to wisdom. Or the journey of god Horus from simpleton child, to fulfilling his destiny. Sometimes I hear you say, 'I am very innocent of things', an innocent and a fool perhaps.

Abraham of Wurms charts his own journey away from ignorance; studying with various teachers, mostly Kabbalists in 15th century Europe. He wants Lamech, after reading his story, to follow in his footsteps. For me, this is the key, the journey."

"The extract you sent, with the names of the Abramelin demons, I was intrigued to read it and find so many Hebrew words. I never really got into the Kabbalah. I have read some books which were good and interesting, but I always thought that the secret of the Kabbalah is kind of obvious, and wondered how people missed it."

"And this is?"

"Firstly, take the word 'ABRA' The letters Abra in Hebrew are - A= א, B= ב, R=ר, A=א together they make the word – אברא which means 'I will create' or 'I will be created,' but it depends how you use it in a sentence and how you pronounce it. The meaning of the word Kabbalah is 'receiving'. There are so many ways to receive, and I suppose that the kabbalah is the way for the Jews to explain gnosis to themselves. If I remember correctly, the Kabbalah emerged around the 12-13th century, which I suppose was still quite new at the time of Abramelin, new and fascinating. I believe that whenever someone is ready to receive, he or she will receive it, and it will be the same information, no matter which path you choose, or that chooses you!

Some Rabbis say that women don't have to study the Kabbalah because they are intuitively 'blessed' with the receiving channel; I think so too. Men like to explore, ask questions and debate, write protocols of how, and what, get prepared. Women just know. Take a woman from any walk of life, magically trained or not, when the time comes to receive, she will, and she will not doubt it, no questions asked."

"The tantrik way in a nutshell."

"The ViniYoga I studied, teaches you that you can practice yoga anywhere and anytime, no matter what is your condition or your surroundings. This is very similar to the Aghori, I think, who find gnosis anywhere around them, in the rubbish and amongst the dead. No need for temples, asharams, flashy garments, and clothes, a new yoga mat, or some fancy meditation. Just be open to receive and you will. Maybe I should join the Aghori?"

"Very interesting insights with which I cannot disagree. Although I think the Aghori go a little too far in their love of ugliness. Our tantra would surely be more sensual, a thing of beauty? But otherwise yes, like the simple Hari Krisnan mantra, simple, uncomplex truth ... I've been singing it all day, made me very emotional, I am very open at the moment.

I read in a little pamphlet I have about this, that some scholars play down the magical aspect of Kabbalah, in favour of a more orthodox, what they think of as a mystical approach. They do this for 'political' reasons. You make me realise that the intuitive, natural, approach, is more me. Come to think of it, that's how Yeats and his wife Georgie did their thing. Did I mention I like their magick? Anyways, in trance, they were receiving, and mostly they did this in their bedroom, which was their magical space, not the charnel house! But going back to Abramelin, tell me more of those words, and the things they mean ... if you would, I'd like that."

From the Magical Grimoire of the Morgan Witches - Abramelin

"Thoughts on some of the Hebrew words in the Abramelin text, from the list Mina made that grouped them according to the decans. I think I 'received' a hidden sentence:

Serep, Kosem, Aluph, Neschamah, Schad, Kohen, Nogah, Ubarim, Istaroth.

Serep (angel) — שרף
Kosem (magician) — קוסם
Aluph (champion) — אלוף
Neschamah (soul) — נשמה
Schad (demon) — שד
Kohen (priest) — כהן
Nogah (Venus) — נגה
Ubarim (fetuses) — עוברים
Istaroth (Ishtar) — אישתר

While writing this names and words, and translating them, a thought came to mind about the practice of magical invocation, what if these words, if put in a certain order, can be used as an invocation to the goddess Ishtar-Inanna, the eight pointed star goddess?

The nine words in Hebrew can be narrowed down to eight:
Ishtar-Venus as one goddess, so:
Serep, Schad,

Ubarim, Neschamah,

Aluf , Kosem,

Kohen

At the top point of the star, sits Nogah-Astaroth or Venus-Ishtar. On her right there's a Serep-angel, who is also the evening star, Vesper.

On her left there's a Schad-demon, the morning star – Lucifer.

In the Middle right point, sits the Ubarim, literally fetuses.

Opposite, at the middle left point, sits the Neschama or the soul.

Bottom right, sits the Aluf, the champion.

Bottom left, sits the Kosem, the magician.

At the bottom, middle point, sits the Kohen, the priest (of the moon) opposite to the goddess.

Thus the Invocation would be:

Ishtar,

Morning star Lucifer,

Evening star Vesper,

Fetuses from the underworld,

Touched by the soul from Heaven,

The champion magician has awakened,

the Priest of the moon

To find the right order for the names, I used the eight pointed star of Chaos, which actually gives me, us, much more opportunities. My original thought, the goal of the invocation, was actually Ishtar, via the moon, sending ripples through the cosmos, which awaken her eight 'names', I don't know what to call them?

Another idea was, that they all burst out at once to all directions from the black void that is in the centre of the chaos star. But Mina loves order, it keeps him together and happy, so I thought hard to find some order in the chaos. (you must remember that we goddesses can be very chaotic at times, sometimes all the time).

So,
There are eight names and seven pathways to invoke Ishtar:

The order of the 8 names:

1– Serep
2– Neschamah
3– Aluf
4– Kosem
5– Ubarim
(Anagrams to Ubarim (עוברים) in Hebrew will be Orvim (עורבים), meaning: crows - messengers, so could be crow-messengers?), – can also mean "passing through"
6– Schad
7– Kohen
8– Ishtar

The Seven Pathways are:
1– Serep-Neschama
2– Neschama-Aluf
3– Aluf -Kosem
4– Kosem- Ubarim
5– Ubarim- Schad
6– Schad-Kohen
7– Kohen - Ishtar

If you draw a Chaos star and follow the pathways, you will draw a horizontal eight, something like the sign for Infinity or mobius loop.

See *Ishtar* Star image that heads this chapter

The Mantra:
Serep neschamah Aluf kosem,
Ubarim shad kohen istara
Before us is Ishtar, the morning star,
Whilst Lucifer & Vesper two pillars make,
Rising in twilight when spirits lurk,
And fetuses of the underworld wait
Touched by Neschamah,
The holy, heavenly soul,
those champion magicians,
will a fiery rod raise,
Awakening the priest of the moon

When I drew the sigil for the invocation, it felt more than just a drawing, it seemed like each line and symbol I put on the paper, gave me back a piece of information, this is something like channeling I suppose. One of them told me something like: "to invoke the goddess and to awake the priest of the moon, there will have to be actual physical connection between the priest and the priestess.

When the date is set for the invocation, from that moment until the invocation itself, there should be no physical contact at all between the priest and priestess, or any other.

All through this channeling, I had this feeling that the priest and priestess are completely different characters to us, to Mina and Miryam. The further I was sucked into the sigil as I drew it, the more I felt Miryam fading away, and something else wanting to come out. A thought crossed my mind, what if the invocation and everything to do with it, the preparation etc, will make Miryam and Mina fade away?

If you remember, on those days when we discussed the invocation, Mina and Miryam didn't really have much to say to each other. It was as if they were taken over by something else. It made me feel a bit uneasy. This is new territory which I know nothing about; which is ok, but it all requires time to think it through, and process the situation.

I know the invocation, once we do it, it will be our breaking point, for good or for ill, and it will open up new doors. But maybe we, I, am not yet ready? I am unsure and trying not to think about it at the moment. I can't even look at the sigil, I don't want to work on it at the moment. I don't know this magic. I need to just let it incubate in me, to absorb it. I'm not going to read any books, so don't even think to suggest any to me, but you can tell me what you think.

I understand better when we just converse, from your stories, poems, pieces of information, they all help me understand what is going on in my head, and maybe my heart. You are a great teacher."

* * *

"I know to continue the work we need some physical connection like Ishtar says. We need to earth things, if only a little, if that makes sense, how to earth things a little? It's a big risk but ok, it might be how it ends, not with a bang, but a whimper. But aside from our meeting, what happens to you, alone then in UK whilst I'm back home, pretending nothing has happened?"

"Brighton, I lived in Brighton for nearly 15 years. I was happy. My Brighton crew are family. They know me as I was, as I am, no questions, just love.

When I came to Brighton I was young and in love and just starting on the path of magic. I didn't know much then, but was always very intuitive, years later, and nothing has changed ... I still feel that I know nothing.

Very soon after arriving I learned that Death was hanging around our home, waiting, so my magic was very different in those days. It was all about postponing death, and how to prolong life.

My other half was dying. Sounds very doomed and sad, but it wasn't really. We challenged death every day, we might have been stupid, but we didn't care. Death was already there, it was just a matter of time. Knowing death is near, we weren't scared, we felt free.

I know it all sounds a bit crazy, and it was, but my man was a very special person, one of a kind, and together, we became one, like yin and yang, one dark, one light, you couldn't tell who was what.

My Brighton crew know me from those days, and it's a bond for life. I was not ready when my man decided to let Death in, he'd had enough and wanted to let go. I respected his wish, but I was crushed, I'd failed him. My magic died with him.

I left, thinking, I'll never come back. For years, I thought I'm a rubbish magician, and a silly witch, but one day something happened, and I realised that when he died, he passed his magic onto me. He was a very mercurial, aquarian minded person, and he gifted me an open mind, and very clear vision into far, far, lands. As a couple, I was the one that would go deep, and he was the one to fly. But from that day, I could do both. I was older, stronger, lighter and darker. I'd become whole again and free.

So I am not alone. I will come to meet you only for the Solstice then return here to Brighton, just in case I need support. My base is my shamanic community, if I need to talk, someone will always be there for me. But my real support comes from my horses, my donkey, my animals. I don't need to talk, but they, the animals, still know what to do, and how to help me process stuff.

It was the horse's power that healed my broken body and shattered soul. It was the donkey power that healed my heart. It was the goats that healed my karma and sparked the ancient fire."

* * *

"Miryam ... a bittersweet story you tell, amazing. I feel I should try to share something too, though it will be pale by comparison. Until I met you I regarded myself as pan-sexual.

Now you ask me what does it mean, pan-sexual? It's my new word, instead of bisexual, means not limited in sexual choice with regard to biological sex, gender, or identity. Crowley was very into the god Pan, which seems about right.

You said that already, somewhere, when we first met, you assumed I was gay. I confess, I have had boyfriends in the past, when I was very young, I liked to think of myself like that character Dil from *The Crying Game*. I even lived with a man for quite a while. He had a dark side, but he seemed to love me and he did help me sort myself out. Saying that reminds me how Crowley abused his boyfriend Victor Neuburg, but how he also made him see a dentist to sort his teeth out and a doctor to fix a, wait for it, varicose testicle, ouch, no resemblance on that score bytheway. But my man could also be very controlling, even a little violent.

Why am I telling you this, is part of me trying to manage

expectations downwards? You already know me as more lunar than solar. But honestly, I probably was never really into sex with men, but ended up doing it anyway. I suppose I was just one of those people who fell in love with a best friend, and they just happened to be a man.

When it ended, it seemed easier to just carry on living in that world. So when my next boyfriend had affairs, I was secretly relieved. Sometimes I'd happily wait for him outside the toilets, the so called cottage, while he picked someone up. He always insisted they pay money, and then he'd give the money to me.

He was tough and sometimes very aggressive. I confess, looking back, I got a vicarious excitement from all that, did it compensate for my own passivity. If we got picked on by queerbashers in the street, he'd turn the tables and give them a beating, he really used to go look for it, he'd attack people. Our relationship ended when it looked like he might turn some of that violence on me, it was time to leave. We parted on good terms, just a few regrets. Looking back, these were probably two of the seminal, no pun intended, let's say, important relationships of my life.

I was drowning in debt when I walked out. I had to move back home, to my parents. A year later I moved on, guess where, to Brighton. Wonder if our paths ever crossed, if you'd been free, would you have found me hot. Studying magick, makes you cross boundaries don't you think? My love of women returned, do you think it ever really went away."

"I think you are hot and sexy, the bisexual and androgynous have a unique sex appeal. I think most of us Baphomet initiates are into androgyny."

"Magick, made me stop caring how people might judge me, although, as you say, I still have a tendency to worry too much about things that don't really matter. At university I was like a mentor or wannabe guru for others. I still had some remnants of my former life as a self-styled revolutionary, still a reluctant activist. I ended up elected as president of the university gay society, probably because noone would do it, and in the end nobody thought I should do it either. The laws may have changed, but the outside world was still pretty hostile.

So in Brighton I was doing my degree at the same time as studying Crowley and trying to join his Typhonian Order, which although I didn't realise until later, was, as an *Order*, moribund. John Symonds *The Great Beast*, that work, it breaks down barriers, makes you confront things, makes you see the judgment of others for what they really are. Instead I found comfort in the line 'Doesn't matter, need not be'. When you become so detached, you don't care about anything, and nothing can get to you. Come out, whatever that is, be open. Ignore the voices that try to judge you or stop you. The forces out there that make you conform, stop you discovering before you have even started, these voices are illusion, they don't really matter. I learnt not to hide.

So I spoke out, one time filling in for a speaker at a student

Jewish Society event. I knew nothing, but they must have sensed something. One of the audience said 'I love you Mina, but I also have to say that according to our book, you are an abomination!'

The ridiculousness of it, I couldn't help but find it funny."

"I can see we are both coming from dark places it seems."

NakedTantra 3 – Kiss of Life – Mid April

So finally we come to our third formal ritual session, both of us with a feeling that things are getting a bit fraught:

"Mina, apologies if I offended the gods, but there's one goddess here she's blue and awake and I forgot what she can be like, so don't piss her off."

"OK, not sure what that is about, but I will try to be sensitive. You mean the goddess Kali appeared to you, and I ignored it, and told you to call it a night and go to bed? Bit patronising I guess."

"Thank you. But mostly, I just can't follow your ideas for the ritual, let me see if I understand you; there are twelve yoginis, each an aspect of the goddess Kali? There are twelve erect phalluses, each of which gets to enter the goddess, thrusting twice?"

"Ah, sounds a bit baroque, but yes, you read my mind, but you might like this. In the yantra diagram you drew, there are twelve phalluses, I could say phalli but that sounds even more silly. So I thought, as you only have one phallus available, that is mine, I enter into each yogini in turn, two thrusts for each."

"Yeah, right."

"Just a thought. Basically, slow but deep thrusts, then we pause. And then either repeat the cycle or do twenty four fast ones, then pause. We keep going like that, as long as we can ... I'm so excited, I might only manage a couple of cycles. Then we feed the yogini's."

"With what?"

"Our love."

* * *

Miryam thru the playlist:

(Homelands – Nitin Sawhney)

The music starts, I started dancing, trying to get your attention, calling you. I need you to see me, to hear me so we can dance together. I brought my little bronze Ganesh, and put it on my NakedTantra altar facing me. Usually I'll put it in the middle of the altar, but for some reason I had it out this way. I think you can see me now, dancing naked, moving with the rhythm, calling you to join me."

(Veneno – Chuy Flores)

"You look at me like in a dream, I am dancing for you, but you look like you are staring into a mirror. I keep dancing."

(Lemon Shining – Kognitif)

"As the music starts, I hear the rhythm, and know I can

salsa to that one, so I do a little salsa steps and moves, and see you smile. But you are still in your own space. Then a thought crosses my mind, maybe you don't get it? Maybe you don't get me? I need to go deeper to see what is going on. Towards the end of the track the music is becoming very trippy, very trancy, so I lie on the bed and trance out with it.

(Cafe De Flore – Doctor Rockit)

"I get up, not dancing yet but moving towards you."

"That song, it always gets us going."

"Finally! you got up and stand next to me. I put my left arm on your shoulder, you put your right arm around my waist tango style, we are dancing to the music. You pull me very close to you. We start touching. I remember your touch on my body and I pull you close to kiss you. We kiss. The universe is holding its breath while we kiss. Everything is flying and circling around us, like a storm is forming around us. We kiss. The kiss of life."

The Kiss

From the *Magical Grimoire of the Morgan Witches*

"A man delights in joining the mouth to that of his beloved not in order to bring himself to any unseemly desire, but because he feels it gives mutual access each to the other's soul, which pour themselves each into the other's body and mingle so together that each of them has two souls and a single soul. Hence a kiss may be called a joining of souls rather than of bodies."

Castiglione, B. (1724). *The Courtier*.

Whilst we may, as initiates, object to the characterization of the noble tantrik tradition as one so focused on sexuality and body magic, because it does have other elements; even so it is difficult to deny that carnal knowledge is pretty central to its gnosis. Thus a recent study was called *The Kiss of the Yogini*.

The kiss in itself, as in the mouth to mouth, rather than cunnilingus or felatio, is often overlooked as one of these important things, as a meditational catalyst in its own right. That is to say, one meditates in a very energized way, visualizing having actual sex with the shakti or if in truth, one may assist the other by gently arousing them as they meditate. The famous YabYum posture might be interpreted this way, or if the female adept visions whilst, to put it bluntly, 'sitting on the face' of her assistant, her Shiva or uttara-sadhaka. The recent TV series *Strange Angel* depicts this as the method used by the Thelemic priestess of the Agape Lodge in 1940s California.

But we have moved on too quickly, and have ignored another important sexual connection that might also lend itself to tantrik gnosis. This would be gnosis whilst kissing or kissing in a very tantrik way. You may wonder if any tantrik texts actually explore the kiss? One's first stop might be the famous *Kama Sutra*, which is not, strictly speaking a tantrik text, thought it seems to have been written in that milieu and thus to take account of those ideas. So in fact, these old texts do discuss kissing, but other than the bare mechanics and a listing of the varieties of kiss, there is little said about the inner states, each might kiss could engender.

In spirit, the Morgan witches were guided to this mystery after many excursions into the shear lustful pleasure of disembodied sex in the imaginarium. Miryam once told Mina that one could get bored with kissing in the end, bored with the whole thing. It could lose its power to deliver gnosis, that is not to say that couples couldn't continue with a happy, convivial sex life, in many cases for years. I asked the author of a book about Sexual Magick about their contention that this kind of magick was usually between established couples. The author agreed that this aspect of their relationship might only persist for a honeymoon period at the beginning, and eventually, the power fades, mostly it would. This could be why, in this spontaneous tantra we practice, known as *sahaja*, the connections in real life can sometimes be fleeting or episodic, although potentially sustained this way over many years. This may be why they are sometimes said to be antisocial. But it also gives them a mythic quality, a *dejavu*, the feeling that one is continually meeting that person over many lifetimes, in different guises, and has been doing this for many cycles of return.

So how did we get to this insight? In our magical space, which we call the imaginarium, we have sex, in order to entertain the spirit that we have drawn into us, as an offering. In one such ritual the Shakti says she wants oral sex, 'French kiss my clitoris', she says, so I do. But later, I ask, just to be clear, can you tell me exactly what you mean by 'French kissing'. And this is what she says:

"You take my face in your hands and bring our heads very close together Your lips touching mine; you open your lips and gently slide your tongue into my mouth. My lips are open waiting for your tongue, we touch, taste, our tongues do a little dance. I catch your tongue with my lips, don't worry I won't bite you. We kiss."

We do this many times in subsequent sessions, sometimes in dreams which we now regularly share, sometimes in visions and rituals, this is what we call our NakedTantra. After one of these, Miryam told Mina, 'open your mouth a little wider'. She's a connoisseur of kissing, whereas some might see it as a means to an end, for Shakti it can be an end in itself. So one has to put aside one's lust of result and enter into the moment. Drink lots of pure water, as one needs hydration for all of these practices. Kissing someone or something, gives it life, and this is like one of the most important and enduring rituals of ancient Egypt, the *Ouphor*, meaning 'opening the mouth'. The old Egyptian rite of 'opening the mouth' (for breathing) was another version of the Breath of life. These are also potentially rejuvenating.

The Tantrik Kiss

(paricumbana 'to kiss heartily', cuusana 'to suck'.)

So what about the kiss in the tantrik tradition, *The Kiss of the Yogini*, is the title of David Gordon White's famous book, that discusses tantric sex in south Asian contexts. Much of the material comes from the Kaula (family) or Nath (Sovereign or Lordly) tradition; which have become more well known to us as tantra. Miryam and Mina both share initiations into the Kaulas and Nathas, who place great emphasis on oral transmission, literally 'fluid messages' as described in the sixteenth chapter of the *Kaula-Jnana-Nirnaya* (Investigation of the doctrines of the Kaulas).

These messages, issued via the 'mouth' of the Yogini, which, in some interpretations is thought of as the yoni of a female adept. Ultimately the source of this Gnostic fluid in the classic theory is the elixir that drips down from the thousand petalled lotus, located in or near the head, the so called sahasrara chakra. In some traditions the Yogi can absorb his or her own elixir by utilising a special technique of inverting the tongue and thus diverting the elixir. So potentially the mouth is a place where these cosmic fluid messages can be intercepted. In Kaula lore, the fluid flows down internal channels and accumulates in the lower 'mouth', in other words, the yoni. Oral transmission via cunnilingus is the antinomian method of classic tantra. That's a theory

So there is a parallelism between the mouth and the yoni that is fairly obvious really. Perhaps the special nature of the Kaula liquid messages diverts us from the equally impressive mysteries of one's physical mouth. The mouth is part of the complex of chakras, and is known as *vishuddi*: the pure one. This power includes that of the voice. The mouth is not merely a homologue of the yoni, and vice versa; it has direct autonomic linkages with the sexual centers. Put simply, a good kiss makes the lingam grow and the yoni open like a moist flower. The mouth is a major erogenous zone, that within, contains several sub-erogenous zones, a whole complex of sensations. There is another tantrik concept related to the marmas or pressure points in oriental lore, points of arousal and points of vulnerability.

So there is a very good reason to linger longer on the actual mouth, something that is shared by all genders, men and women and thus could be said to be transgenderal. Should we accept the idea that the female body is the only source of these messages, or, rather that men and women have an internal yogini, described by Jung as one's animus / anima? So we can avoid lust of result and see the ecstasy and fluid messages transmitting in deep kissing, as an end in themselves.

Here ends brief excursus into the mysteries of kissing.

Kiss of Life Ritual (continued)

(Eternal Ending – Keybe, Agartha & Dali Triki)

"We crashed on the bed. I need some rest, my heart is racing

we smoke a joint, I'm diving into deep trance."

(Emerald Rush - Jon Hopkins)

"We are still on the bed, I want to get up, I like this track, but I can't move."

(Infinite Space – Stanisha)

"You spread my legs open. I can feel your breath on my yoni, your tongue licking me, your lips sucking my clit."

"Slowly and gently

Slowly and gently

Slowly and gently

I need to dance to this one. I get up and dance, very trancy sounds. I go very, very deep. I trance dance, I'm somewhere else. I'm writing to you now and it's all coming back to me. The mare is riding the deep black waves of the ocean. I am lost in music, I'm gone. I dance a very sexy and sensual dance. My yoni is so close to your lingam, I can feel you inside. I open my eyes and see Ganesh staring at me, he is glowing in the dark. We are connected in some strange rays of light."

(Karma – AIWAA)

"I crash onto the bed again. I need to close my eyes for a few seconds. My mind is racing, feeling like I'm observing something that is going on in my bedroom, in myself. The only way to work it out, is to trance out some more, so I smoke a little more."

(Celeste – MiRET)

"I Love this track. Time to work out what is going on, I get up and I dance. The rhythm of horses cantering and the crazy violin get my heart racing and my head flying. I'm a naked cowgirl dancing with her horses, riding her sea mare. The mare and I are at the edge of the void; it is full of shining stars. We fly above it and nosedive into the stars."

(Ederlezi "Spring Festival" in the Romany tongue
Goran Bregovic [Jack Essek edit])

"It's a song about thanksgiving, so I thank all the powers that came down into my bedroom and helped. 'I Thank You, Spring has come!' It is time to wake up and live a little."

(Nel Blu – Floex)

"Probably my favorite track of the last two years. This song is so me; the rhythm, the hypnotic vibe and voice, my dreams, the feeling of being swept off my feet. It is opening my heart, wide open. This is the sound of my magic, Can you hear it?"

(Wolf & I – Itom Lab)

"I sing and howl
You are the wolf
I am the moon
…

In my dreams
wolf & I"

   (Galactic Mantra – Itom Lab)

"I had to bring Baphomet into the Umbra Zonule.
I am Me
We are You."

"Dearest Miryam

Amazing record. Not sure I can match that but I feel very much with you.

Putting Ganesh in the ritual, not sure we ever discussed that beforehand, so came as a bit of synchronicity, a shock of recognition. Ganesh is very special to me, as he is to you, obviously. When I read that, I thought it must be some kind of message, how could I have forgotten him after all these years together. Singing that mantra, made me so happy – *Om Gan Ganepatayeh namo namah, Shara gan ganesha*.

After that I started the playlist like we said. At first I just sat, expecting you to come in vision and after that we would adopt a fairly static posture, but it wasn't like that.

As soon as the music started, I see you arriving, naked but wanting to dance. I remember you said you don't much like meditating, you prefer to move, like a shaman? So we do, like Shiva and Shakti, I remember we danced quite a lot.

From the sweat and grime on our bodies we can made this magical child, which is how, in the story, Ganesh also got made. Sometimes we touched each other very intimately. Like in the ritual before, we enjoyed a very long, Gnostic kiss, but all the time still dancing, or bodies closer and exciting each other, but still we kept on. Sometimes we fell on the ghadi (bed) and felt each other, but then again the music picks us up and we dance.

I remember I lay down, as in yoga nidra, I slept and must have dreamt, a nightmare, waking in terror, as I often do. I saw a demonic figure, its color like that of the plasma on the computer. There was a snake which someone, me, someone else, snared with a cord, deftly looping it around its neck until it stopped writhing, and was hanging and dead.

'kill your own snakes' I said aloud. So I did it, although I know it won't be the last of them. I am 'Eros with graying temples'.

When we meet, you say we should do all this dance meditation somehow in truth. Are we really going to dance naked, to come forth by day in front of the whole world? Perfect love and perfect trust, will I, will we, really do that ... ? "

Later

"Mina. I think the nightmare is the most important of dreams, not just for you, but for everyone. They make you pay attention. I had one too. Something has definitely shifted in the way I dream.

"I'm driving my car, another car is driving towards me in my lane, for a split second our eyes meet. It is you, you see me too and you drive your car towards me. It looks like we are going to crash into one another, but I know we won't. You stop your car just in time. We are sitting in our cars and looking at each other. I say 'you look so real' and reach over to touch your face through the windscreen, just as you pull me to you. We are sitting now, in a big dining room, something like you'd see in a Kibbutz. All I can remember is repeatedly saying 'that you look so real'. You're are wearing your red shirt. I touch your hand and you are.

Are you for real?

Who are you?"

Lover's Story

"People are ridden by their Zar spirits, like horses, it's all very personal at first, like an illness or condition. There are horses of the zar, like there are horses of voodoo."

"One of my dogs killed a chicken earlier and now it has brought the head to my door so I can do some voodoo spells with it..."

"So can I sneak into your bed tonight."

"You'd be welcome, you really want to cuddle me up?"

"Only if you cuddle me first."

"So what would make you happy tonight?"

"Lie naked on top of me and do deep love kissing."

"We kiss. My tongue in your mouth, playing with yours.

But whatever you do, no hot, wet fanny hovering over my cock!"

"But I'm lying on top of you, of course you're gonna feel

my hot wet fanny!"

"I have to spread my legs a little so I can get more comfortable."

"I might get a bit hard if you do that. I'm into the kissing but your fanny is right over me now. I can feel the lips opening, you better not slide over me."

"You can kiss me while I'm sliding over you very gently, hovering over your cock. Don't stop kissing me."

"My heart misses a beat, catching my breath, you better not wank yourself on my cock or I'm going to die. You're sliding your fanny up and down on me. Oops, I in you."

"Up and down on your cock, each time a little bit deeper. We're still kissing, sometimes I'll kiss your ears, sometimes your neck, and then your lips again."

"Oh gawd! Mina wants Miryam so bad now, better just fuck now."

"We fuck, but do you want to go for a ride?"

"Just fuck me, I want those hot fanny walls squeezing my cock. I'm not thrusting but I might just explode with cum inside you soon. Groaning with lust. Mina loves Miryam. You can ride on the horn of the unicorn."

"I'm up and down, moving fast and then slowing down squeezing you from inside kissing you with both my lips, mouth and fanny. I love your unicorn horn, I think I might just come."

"I think I might just be coming too."

"I want to feel you exploding in me."

"I feel it coming, pulsing, then a fountain inside you, your fanny twitching, grasping, you can't be sure who is who. Arching and pushing within for union. All reflexes now."

"Floating."

"Holding each other very close."

"Heart to heart."

"Little kisses."

"Breathing."

"Good night my love."

"Dream whole thing again now, but no making me come. ;)"

"I can't promise that."

Later

"Amazing tantric night, doing the same, over and over. My dreams are of rising very high on a skylift, flying dreams. Do I have a fear of flying?"

"They say, that when we fly in our dreams, we are growing, physically, mentally, and spiritually. You are learning to lose control and fly. Fly with me."

Chapter 5
Behemoth, the elephant

Magical record of the Morgan witches

"Sweet Mina, You really don't see it do you. What we do, you and I is recapturing the sweetness of youth. I asked you once to think of all the lovers in myths and tales of the old times to see if you can see us, now I want you to think what are they trying to tell us with their stories of dancing, kissing,

---

Predynastic slate makeup palette, Egypt

fucking, 'Eternal fornication' as you call it, and what for if not to teach us the secrets of eternal youth, Eternal love.

Visualisation exercise

Listen to *Cafe de Flore* and read all this again:

"Finally! you got up to stand next to me. I put my left arm on your shoulder, you put your right arm around my waist tango style, we are dancing to the music. You pull me very close to you. We start touching. I remember your touch on my body, and I pull you close to kiss you. We kiss. The universe is holding its breath while we kiss. Everything is flying and circling around us, like a storm is forming around us. We kiss. The kiss of life."

See us kissing.

Feel the world standing still around us and at the same time circling us like a tornado. After you've done that, I think you'll have some answers

* * *

"Dearest Miryam,

OK, here's one that popped into my memory after doing all that":

Behemoth, the elephant
Masaylama the prophet,
Called false by the Muslims,
Knew the use of perfumes,
by which a man,
and woman,

excite the act of copulation.
He knew the secrets of the Elephant,
Behemoth in the Bible,
whose strength reaches its peak on the summer solstice,
when he lets out a loud roar,
making all ferocious animals quake with fear,
keeping them civilized for the year,
So they leave the others alone.
That Behemoth goes where he wills,
Eating grass like an ox,
But strength is in his loins,
and force is in his navel
his cock is like wood,
His balls pulled up by the sinews when aroused,
his bones are like bars of iron.
He is the chief of the ways of God:
who has made him like a sword,
to plunge into a sheaf.
The mountains bring him food,
& all beasts of the field will play.
While he lies under shady trees,
or among the reeds and fens,
drinking up a river,
then slow and steady, he will fuck his mate
until the end.
But then Masaylama met Khadija the prophetess.
She went to test him out,

Hearing that when women smell his perfumes,
they swoon and throw themselves into his arms,
and say do it every way with me.
So she wrote him a letter,
saying she would examine him,
and he should examine her.
And she sealed the letter with her own menstrual blood,
knowing it would send him mad with desire.
When Masaylama opened the letter,
His mind was full of confusion.
She was coming, whether he willed it or not.
So he erected a pleasure tent,
of beautiful brocades,
filled with couches and sofas,
fit for the ways of love.
And in it he wafted his most beautiful perfumes,
Amber, musk,
and flowers, like yonis,
roses, hycinth, carnations, and lotus,
and censers with aloes, and nard that smells of lust,
vapors strong enough to impregnate water.
When she comes and inhales my perfumes,
she will delight, all her bones will be relaxed,
in soft repose,
and she will swoon before me,
All our troubles fade away,
And we will possess each other.

Khadija the prophetess came into the tent,
and as predicted,
all her troubled thoughts drifted,
and though confused she thought only of sex.
Masaylama seeing her arousal,
asked how she wanted it?
Lie down on your back and I will pleasure you,
first with kisses and tinkles,
licking your yoni and entering you with firm
but gentle strokes.
Or place yourself on all fours,
as if praying,
your fanny thrust backwards,
I shall squeeze into your yearning wetness,
and pleasure you ...
Khadija the prophetess replied,
I want it done all ways,
let the revelation of the divine fall upon us,
Prophet of the divine.
Enter me ... and I shall anoint you cock with,
my own ejaculation and moonly blood,
And when I am totally done,
you will ask me for marriage.
And when,
after a very long time,
she left the tent,
the flush of love on her cheeks,

Her disciples gathered and asked,
How went the conference,
Oh Prophetess of god?
And she said, her voice quivering still,
Maysalama has revealed to me,
& I to him.
The Truth we found,
comes down to you,
To you all,
Miryam and Mina.

"Mina, good far-memory you retrieved there. Changing the subject. Can you imagine that there are people in the world who will not kiss. A friend came to visit yesterday. We go way back, about 30 years. She is probably what some might call 'my best friend'.

Anyway, she got herself tangled in some weird relationship, and told me she is very sexually frustrated with this man, he is not listening to her needs, too shy or maybe just too hung up on religious practice, anyway, she is not happy. She knows about you and our sexy thingy, not in detail, just the idea. She is always fascinated with my 'stories'. I never tried to 'convert' her into anything, she is different to me personality wise, and this balances me.

Gosh I talk too much... I'll try to get to the point. When she was talking about her lover, a question popped into my mind, which I had to ask her, 'Do you kiss?' I asked her. And she said, he never kissed her, he never kisses. Apparently this is something to do with his religious practice, which I found complete bullshit, as he is more then willing to have sex with her!

This brought on some gnostic discussion about The Kiss – The Kiss of life, which made me really proud of her, she has listened to all my ranting and bullshit over the years, she understands! I shared with her my instructions to you about how to kiss. The realisation and understanding of what is going on with her and her lover, hit her big time, she was in tears. I sent her home with some homework, she will listen to the playlist 'The Breath of Life' and to write down her feeling on each track, especially about Cafe de Flore."

"Dearest Miryam, I can't imagine a religious rule against kissing! I never heard of that. I wonder whether that might also be a gender thing at work, women being more into that, and men, by conditioning or nature, less oral? You could do a survey, but I have also heard of people who reserve that, that's something else, but sex but not kiss, too intimate?"

"From my point of view, I have heard even stranger tales, concerning the sexual habits of the more, let's say socially conservative types. They seem so unlike Masaylama and his lover in the old story you remembered. How things have changed. Just one example, not sure how typical it is, but it happens, and to me it shows the prisons people sometimes make for themselves. Another friend, told me how his wife suddenly changed when she became more religious. The thing that bothered him the most, was the way she used to 'clean' herself before and after sex. He said it got to the point where she couldn't have sex unless both were 'properly' clean, so they had to have a shower. I can understand how having a shower is nice, but then, you know, sometimes you just want to do it and you don't care about anything else. And what really got to him, was that the second he'd come, she would jump out of bed, and go and wash herself. She made him do the same. But he said it made him feel like she was washing him off. Which perhaps she was."

"I love your stories, the memories of previous times, things that you are doing, don't worry about going off on one, say more, whenever you like, you write so well too. And, for future reference, in another life, if ever you want to seduce Mina, then offer him a kissing session. I can't resist a good snog. Do you think it is just the religious people who are so uptight? I say religious, but we're religious, strictly speaking, I'd say so. But I know when people say religious these days, they mean a certain mindset, a more restrictive thing."

Orthodox Jews practice Negiah, touch or touching, it means that from the first day of the woman's menstruation, for about two weeks, the week of her period and another week after, her husband will not touch her, not even touch her hand. This sounds a bit strange to us. Myself, I would not want to practice anything like that. But, I have heard many orthodox women saying that this way, it actually helps with the sex for the days after. But, apart from the time of the Negiah, I never heard of Jews not being allowed to kiss."[1]

"Which brings me to the answers I got via your liquid messages. You were on top, I'm inside you. You are in control and move quite fast, churning and whirling on my erect lingam. You are so strong inside, possessed by the spirit of the submarine mare. You get wilder and wilder, churning, churning the ocean. I need to relinquish control to you but I still have a residual fear, will she break me, crush me. But then we are churning together, then coming inside each other. I feel the warm glow all night, the after effect of our churning/whirling. I felt this very much in the sexual centre, the one the Hindus call *svadhisthana* which I learn means "one's very own place". It's surely more than overt arousal or satiation, a constant vibrancy, thought I'd mention that. How did you feel?"

"Sometimes, all this leaves me feeling so very open and

---

[1] "Within Judaism there is what you call Negiah – Negiah Hebrew: נגיעה – literally "touch", is the concept in Jewish law (Halakha) that forbids or restricts physical contact with a member of the opposite sex (except for one's spouse outside the niddah period, and certain close relatives to whom one is presumed not to have sexual attraction). A person who abides by this halakha is colloquially described as a shomer negiah ("one observant of negiah").The laws of negiah are typically followed by Orthodox Jews, with varying levels of observance. Some Orthodox Jews follow the laws with strict modesty and take measures to avoid accidental contact, such as avoiding sitting next to a member of the opposite sex on a bus, train, airplane, or other similar seating situation. Others are more lenient, only avoiding purposeful contact. Adherents of Conservative and Reform Judaism do not follow these laws (Wikipedia)

raw, so naked. After our churning and whirling I was drained and a little empty. My body responded with bleeding, my period, which is not so regular at the moment. It's more about responding to things around me, all those insights I'm having, it makes me realise, that I could go without sex, probably forever if needed. But, without a kiss, that would be something else ... I can't imagine that.

Running on empty
(From Mina to Miryam)

Running on empty
Just fumes in the tank,
Better stop, fill up,
with something from bank,
the well, of inspiration,
that never runs dry,
So they say, but there again,
sometimes it just does.
So we meet in your bedroom,
And do it all again,
Sharing the breath of life,
As Horus & Seth shared it,
As Thoth & Horus shared it,
Their feet resting on the lungs,
The windpipe stretched up between them,
Papyrus and lotus fronds weaving,
A mysterious pattern,
Around their bodies.

The in and the out breath,
Mouths devouring each,
Tongues gripped and searching,
All our body's parts melding together.
The heart, the stomach,
The sexual centre,
Full of elixir now,
Lingam and Yoni touching,
Then over and in each,
Floating, in mysterious lands,
A plateau through the hours of darkness,
Coming forth at daybreak,
Refreshed & inspired,
Well within us now.

"Mina, This is beautiful, you have put into your own words, what is going on in my mind, in my heart. I knew you would understand. You know that when people read this, it will open their mind to a whole new way of thinking. The gnostic tantra?
'Wild thing.
you make my heart sing'."

Dream control by sexual magick

Miryam wraps her tongue around Mina's lingam three and a half times and clamps her mouth over him. As he is about to come, she gentle touches a secret pressure point, telling him reassuringly, 'don't faint.'

'I'll come in your mouth?"

"I'll drink your sweet elixir."

Dreams

Around midnight, it's quiet, the household has settled for the night. Then our dog, gets all spooked and starts barking at nothing, which is not really like him. I hear one of the people in the house stirring in his room and, unusually for him, as he sleeps through almost everything, but now he is going down to see what is making the dog bark.

Dream #1

I was in the primal landscape which is the one where I was brought up. I was in the house of Malcolm Lee, a childhood friend, a descendent of Babbacombe Lee, 'The Man they couldn't Hang', or so he said. There was a stranger, an intruder in the house. It was the fear that woke me, the ominous feeling that someone was there. I hear a crash from upstairs, it sounded like you, like Miryam. I call out, and went to look, but the rooms are eerily deserted. Someone is at the door. I peer at them through the frosted glass, trying to make out their features. Their hair is short, but I still think it is you. I decide not to open the door just the same.

I woke up, got up and wrote it all down. Then I sent a late

night message. I undressed again and went back to bed. I must have fallen asleep only to wake from another dream. This time I have an erection, someone is there, I'm anxious until I see it is you, Miryam, but this time dressed in a red saree. You look different, could even be Asian. I look closer, I can definitely tell it is you. You tell me you are studying in a college, it's the break, when the students move between classes. You are not happy there, you want to change, the other students don't like you. You take me to your bedroom, although this is strictly against the rules. Your father is in the room next door, if he hears us he will be very angry. You tell me your father is a demon, an Asura, that you are descended from the Asura. You are a feminine kind of demon, an Asuri. She was the demoness who suckled the ancient philosopher Kapila, and through her breast milk passed her gnosis to him. I know your father has a demonic face, if he finds us he will yell 'What are you doing in my daughter's room unsupervised.' Demons are sticklers for protocol. You tell him, he shouldn't worry, because you are still a virgin, we're just talking, nothing we say will change that."

Next day

"Was that the G-spot you touched. I mean, do men have a G-spot as some say women do? Correction, some say they do and some say they don't, is it all just a legend? I read somewhere that a man and woman's sexual anatomy are actually very similar, although obviously organized differently? Look at the anatomy of the clitoris, including the parts behind the scenes. It could be almost the same size as all the bits of a penis added together, but more of it is inside the woman's body!"

"Mina, all I can say is that sometimes the whole vulva is one big G-spot, this part of a woman's body is very sensitive, they are blessed. Though I know most women find that their clitoris is the most sensitive part, but for many, it's the penetration that does it for them, because sometimes, what's inside, is more sensitive. Don't you remember the old times? Let's incubate another dream tonight."

Next Day

"My first dream was yet another nightmare, so many of those. I'm in the house of my father, when there is a complete power outage, plunging us into pitch black. What is the message here. Later that night. I found you on the shore of a large salt water lagoon. The water was so blue, but we're not alone. I'm wearing cut-off jeans held up with a broken clasp. You tell me I should just take them off as they're falling anyway. The beach is not deserted, I'm self conscious. We move into the water together and I let them go, so we're both naked in the water together. I remember you told me something about becoming lucid but I've forgotten what it is I'm supposed to do, so I just keep swimming next to you, not quite touching, until, eventually, I wake up."

"What does the house of the father mean to you?"
"My father, filial but also an archetype, in Jungian sense

of it. He often shows up in my visions when I need some protection or a sanctuary. Perhaps his house will play some role in our story, be a sanctuary of some kind? I thought, these days he is the one more in need of my help. But in the past, he was usually there for me. The light failing like that, he could be in trouble, although, and this is unusual for me, in the complete black out, it was ok. I may be scared but I go on, all the way to the necropolis."

"Or him accepting death. Like I said before Mina, it is vital for our work to work with nightmares, so I need you to help me on this one, and try to remember every detail you can. It can be the tiniest detail that you think is not important, that is the key to it all. The blue lagoon, that was a success, from my point of view. That feeling, on the beach, of not being alone, I'd been suggesting that to you in my head all day. And when you started questioning stuff in a dream, when you are aware of yourself and actually acting on it, like when you said 'I let them go ... we're both naked in the water', that is lucid dreaming, once you get the hang of it, you can actually change your dreams ... and nightmares. I will try to be quiet and not get under your skin for the next few days, but you know me, I can't promise you that, but I will try."

"The lagoon was in the desert or coast, great clouds of salt crystals around the shore, the water clear and the temperature the same as our blood. The water, ice blue, is so beautiful. Being naked in the water was very erotic, I felt my idealised self, in the waters. I am beautiful, my skin lightly tanned, moving through the water. We are naked together, I feel … well you know. *The Perfumed Garden* says one cannot have complete sex in water, but it a very sensuous."

"Nonsense, these old books don't always know. The colour tells you this is lucidity. Hold me and bury yourself in me.

So many secrets

The breath of life we found, is coming from many cultures and many paths, and probably they all share it. You told me about the opening of the mouth ritual in ancient Egypt, also the Bible when God breathed on Adam to give him life, hence the magic of giving life to a man shaped from clay. There is also a nice myth about the Prana which I remembered from Yoga school and found it online:

The Chandogya Upanishad

Once the five Senses, Hearing, Sight, Smell, Taste and Touch were sitting around, they talked about all the things they could do. The Senses were somewhat boastful about their abilities and importance and they claimed to be the rulers of the body. Look at us, for we are remarkably special, they claimed! There is no way the body survives without us, they boasted.

Each sense, in turn, showed off its abilities. Hearing filled the space with music that breathed emotion and passion that stirred the soul. Sight matched the music with a breathtaking splendor of swirling, magical forms in exquisite shades of colours. Smell, in a puff of breath, perfumed the expanse with heavenly aromas. Taste, not to be outdone, exhaled out a cornucopia of mouthwatering flavours. Touch made the whole body vibrant with each and every breath, tingling with soft warmth and delicious coolness. They all lavished praise for one another. It was quite a show.

Prana quietly breathed in and out, watching this awesome spectacle. It was simply there, present. With the in-breath, it observed the Senses; with the out-breath, it observed the Senses. After letting the Senses go on for a while, Prana said, "None of you reigns supreme in the body." No one was listening. The Senses had no time or awareness of anything else. They were completely blind to everything beyond themselves and certainly had no sight of Prana. Prana tried again. The Senses, in their total self absorption, had no attention to spare for Prana. Angered, Prana left.

As Prana left, the sounds, colours, fragrances, tastes, physical sensations, and the mind, all faded and disappeared. The Senses ceased to exist. The Senses had no idea of what happened. As Prana returned, they found themselves and knew that they were. Prana left and the Senses were no longer there. The Senses were suddenly vulnerable and scared.

Prana reappeared and suddenly they were aware of Prana. Like a light switch, they were turned on and off by this vital energy over which they had no control, but the energy had total control over them. With this awareness came the instant realization that they existed because of Prana and that this vital energy was far more powerful than them. They did not rule the body at all in any way. Prana did.

As they bow down in respect, Prana told them, "Dividing myself five times and spreading out in the body, I change my form and create the Senses from myself and thus give life in the body."

Another session, a long discussion of freedom, which irritates Miryam so much until she says, sarcastically: 'Do you still want to kiss me?' But Mina ignores her and continues talking about freedom and how it is available to a 'householder' like him, like they both are. This is different to the kind of freedom enjoyed by a total renouncer, a sannyasin. Freedom, yes, but with limits, sometimes physical, sometimes financial, material, but to ignore all this is hubris. All freedom has limits. Only in the imaginal realm can one truly be free.

"I want Mina back."

"I guess you are seeing my personality."

"I want Mina back"

Lover's Story

"My horn shalt thou exalt like the horn of a unicorn: I shall be anointed with fresh oil"
(Psa. 92.10.AV).

"Mina?"

"I'm here."

"Kiss me!"

"I will."

"How will you kiss me, Tell me?"

"A half tantric kiss tonight, but still a little bit sexy. Let me kiss you better."

"I'd like that."

"I hold your face in my hands. I kiss your eyes, your nose. My lips on your lips. My tongue licking your lips, opening them and sliding inside your open mouth. Our tongues meeting, greeting, dancing. You suck on my tongue. I suck you too."

"It's all so very dark around us. There's only a kiss. Shining through our hearts, illuminating the night, Giving us life."

"I never been kissed quite like you do."

"Kiss me, You know how."

"You taught me …"

"So show me what you learned."

"This is half tantric kiss, remember, don't get carried away. Sucking your tongue, then you suck mine, mouths so moist and yearning, lips, erogenous. Eating each other, almost, we're definitely going to get carried away, can I feel you as we kiss, just a little."

"Put your arms around me, feel my heart, feel me. Slide those beautiful hands of yours over my thighs and between my legs. I miss you."

"I won't stop kissing, my hand is on your inner thigh. What are you wearing?"

"A caftan, take it off if you like, gently."

"Let's kiss more. I can feel your fanny, hold my cock, you're pretty wet down there, my fingers open your labia a little and rest there."

"This is all bliss."

"I love the way you feel."

"Yes."

"I missed you."

"My left hand touching your face, your cock is in my right hand. Our kiss, breathing life into our tired bodies, into your cock, into my yoni, which is wet, and hot, and waiting for your fingers."

"Your legs open, my right hand is on your fanny, touching the inner lips which are wet like our mouths."

"Perfect circuit, don't let it stop."

"Your fanny lips open and my fingers are slipping just inside you. Then out again, glistening with moisture. I can feel your clitoris wants to be touched."

"I suck on your tongue, licking your lips, kissing you. Your fingers touching,

I touch your hand and guide you. Touch my clit and maybe push your finger in, a bit deeper."

"My middle finger glides over your clit then pushes deep inside, so I can feel the walls of your vagina pulsing, again and in, finger fucking you. I touch myself and am licking my fingers."

"My wet hand on your cock, I move it gently and squeeze it a little. I can feel it hard in my hand. I want you."

"Vagina lips squeeze my finger. I can feel you. You want to ride me as we sleep, until we sleep? All night. I'll be waiting."

"Lie down and I will sit on your unicorn horn."

"I'll lie down, you can slide down my horn and gently fuck me all night."

"I will love you gently all night."

"Yes, whisper secrets to me as we merge, rest and keep rejoining."

"I will. I'm sorry I was moody today."

"Sexual healing now."

"Yes. Our thing."

"Woke up with an orgasm!"

"Wow, I love that."

"Yes, so did I. We were very busy last night."

Chapter 6
Vampires
(late May)

Do you believe in magic?

When the air is warm, the sky clear, & the stars are out, I believe in magick. When the rain is falling & darkness descends, our magic is strong

---

Nofret, wife of Rahotep high priest of Heliopolis, vivid well preserved polychrome sculpture from Egypt's IVth dynasty, pyramid age, superb art of very high standard. Could be models for Anne Rice's mother & father of all Vampires, "those who must be kept."

Vampires
(from the Magical Grimoire
of Morgan Witches)

"Is it our love making that attracts the spirits? If so, that would be a very ancient dynamic. We must take care to filter, to allow through only those who can teach us what we need to know. Men and women, especially women, can get very sexy in their heads and can feel it in their bodies, even if there is no physical partner present.

We took an oath to work this magick for a year and a day. Soon we will actually meet, face to face, in the flesh, but it is strange to read through our grimoire, and remind ourselves of all the things we did, even before that. This is an experiment in magic, I don't know what kind of magic you call it but one thing I do know, we are magickal partners, we have to remember that, even when we get carried away, so far and deep, but that's magick.

Love is a magical thing, probably the most magical magic one can think of. It can come in all sorts of ways and shapes, we need to just let it be what it wants to be, to be ourselves, let it reveal itself to us."

"It could be that psychological pain of loneliness & separation is part of the ground condition of this magick. The yearning for physical union of the flesh gets almost unbearable sometimes. When lovers meet after such a preliminary, there is sure to be an explosion of desire, especially for the man. Sometimes it is like an illness or a pain, that craves release, one's sexual centre, as the Hindu's called the svadhisthana, literally the city of jewels, feels so gravid and heavy. In the flesh, there is such a backlog of lust, the meditation, as we have come to call it, maybe won't last for as long as it does in the imaginarium."

Miryam, smiling, thinks to herself, Mina is preparing me for wonderful, ecstatic sex that will last a few seconds the first time he explores her yoni with his lingam.

"*Morning shower insight.* We, you and I, have certain aspects of Vampirism in us. We are feeding on each other's thoughts, ideas and sexual energy. It is very consuming and tiring. The logical thing to do is to stop feeding off each other. But if we stop feeding, it will all fizzle out and die, for above all this, we are vampires. So no feeding, no energy, no sex, no magick. There is no logic to this sort of magic, we need to feed to sustain what we have, and grow further. The Kiss of life, the Breath of life, talking, writing, dreaming, even kissing; this is the way we feed; circular breath, that moves from you to me, and vice versa. There will be a time when we will feed less, or maybe even fast, but to keep this thing, this magic we create, we need to keep feeding. We only feed on each other, I don't see the point on feeding on others. So we are vampires, we go on forever, remember that. The problem is that our last feed was such a long time ago, too long. It has left us both feeling strange. On Saturday I will meet you in our cave, on the lovely bed you put there for us. We will listen to the Stillness playlist and breathe.

Remember the two fish? 'Like two fish, I suck you as you suck me' only when we do it that way, maybe we don't suck each other dry? When we meet, in the flesh, at Glastonbury, it might well be that we are so revivified, that we cannot stop!"

"Miryam, we said a year and a day, knowing full well that we would have to separate one day. Part of me thinks the most logical moment to separate would be after our reunion in Glastonbury, which is fast approaching. Will our tomb remain empty after that, like those in Egypt, which are often empty, abandoned, but full of memories of forgotten loves, or of meetings that never were? We may come to see it that way, which makes the time remaining all the more precious, we will use it wisely but, even so, we must also ease off, a little, for the sake of our wellbeing, so as not to suck each dry."

"Lets go sleep in our cave again tonight, together."

"My demon lover, I agree with what you say. We feed from each other, it is not just me, or either of us vamping the other. It is mutual, we feed from each other, equally. Sometimes tiring, crazy, always inspiring, and, I have to admit, pleasurable ... A sweet kiss goodnight for now."

Later

"What you wrote made me dream of our cave, which I saw as a multiplex cinema. In one room I found a proof version of our Book of Life. The pages are very colourful, printed in raised flock or velvet printing. We've been living inside the magick lantern, the fantasmagoria, but soon it is time to leave, before returning to our native lands. There are others watching, they see our gold and make plans to steal it. But we see what they are doing and trick them, so all they get it a plastic copy of our pure gold coin."

Aleister Crowley Comes
(from Grimoire of Morgan Witches)

...Binah, the supernal understanding, is connected with Tiphereth, the Human Consciousness, by Zain ... Intuition. Crowley, *Liber ABA*

"When you know that Zain, is how in Hebrew, one refers to a phallus, then the whole makes sense as body magick, as NakedTantra !

I just woke up and it is already 38 degrees! I don't try to channel Aleister Crowley, I never thought about him, not really, although these last few days, after reading your post about the Museum of Witchcraft and Magick, and how its founder really liked him, I did read some. Like many others, you seem to be obsessed with him, no wonder he still has power ... My thoughts might sound like heresy, but I can't help thinking that maybe Crowley had a different agenda altogether, and was taking all of you for a ride? Was he taking the piss out of his followers?

If so, then this is the sad, inevitable feature of the whole cult scene, can you think of any examples where this isn't the way of all gurus?

I know nothing about it really, just the occasional article I read but only if it's not too long. And of course his *Book of Thoth*, the Tarot cards which I love but still hardly use. Saying that, I think that what he wrote about the fool, gave me an idea of a new way to work the Tarot. I do think it's sad that he is counted almost as a demon, what do you think about this status? Did the link we created, in which you bring your relation to Crowley, and I, my keys to the otherworld, made a gap for him to slip in? He is not bothering me really, I am just aware of him around us. Should I or we do something about it?"

"Since his death, Aleister Crowley is indeed mostly treated as a demon, rather than as the spirit of a master that one should continue to channel. According to the recent talk you refer to, Gerald Yorke helped Cecil Williamson with his project, though he thought he may have become obsessed by the demon Crowley. I think this is also known as 'The ordeal of the demon Crowley', for obvious reasons. It can of course be a useful source of information, but it can also lead to obsession if he gets too close. I'm not trying to put you off, but just so you have the right information. It's partly because he sets up such expectations, especially for 'one to follow him', that is to say, a magical child to fulfill his mission. What a trip that would be, but also what a poison chalice. Anyway, with the right framing, it can be useful. Given the kind of magical energy we are trying to work with, I wouldn't be at all surprised if he is in the air. I don't think we should block him, but perhaps listen, and see what he wants, or what he can offer, to the work."

"I woke up today and remembered the astral travel dream work I did a few years back, so I looked it up and realised my dream was a journey about the two Tarot cards, the Lovers and Art. Crowley remade the old Temperance card, turning it into Art, which he says is how it was always meant to be.

You know, before I go, I have to say, looking at the old pictures of Crowley, there is a resemblance, to you I mean. Anyways, at the time, I couldn't see what the dream really meant. So here's what I wrote in my diary, some years ago:

Atu VI – The Lovers;

Atu XIV – Art

Two cards, one journey (it was an exercise in astral travel). The two cards together represent the alchemical marriage, the death of the individual, into the Orphic egg, the void. The black arm is pouring fire into the cauldron, while the white arm is pouring the gluten like substance into the mix. Together they are a new form, the androgynous body and mind, the paradox of the left and right in one body. The creation of a new ideal shape, a new way of life: Solve et Coagula.

Last night, for whatever reason, (was Aleister Crowley lurking in the dark?) I had to look at the Atu VI – The lovers. This card was always a bit of a mystery to me. I understood it intellectually, but hadn't seen the dream potential. I think I can see it now, it is very much describing the work of the

Morgan Witches – two bodies merging into one, one mind dreaming. Two hands, my right hand, your left hand, making it happen."

"Do you use the Crowley deck a lot? The lovers is such an alchemical thing, like the Möbius strip placed over their outstretched hands, as they grope in the darkness, initiates, seeking knowledge, this time via the mysteries of the sacred marriage."

"Just let the alchemy, as you call it, do it's work. I'm just the vessel which collects the information. Remember what I wrote about 'Release Control': *'We are still in deep trance but back in our bodies now. We breathe into a deeper trance, releasing control. Breathe my love.' The only way to really have me, is when you release control, and surrender to the flow of love, that will heal us.' I put my hand in yours, we are lying on our backs, side by side, my right hand holding your left hand. We are spiraling down the rabbit hole.*

What did Aleister Crowley do that was so terrible? Was it the sacrifice of animals, the sex, did he kill people? I don't really understand ... animal sacrifice, you find that in many paths, same for sex, so what made him so outrageous compared to others? I'm just trying to understand the myth that has been created around him. What do you think of him?"

"I think love-hate, he is just part of me now. He gave me my first adventures in hyperreality via his books, especially *Liber ABA Magick* which I read in my hometown, smalltown, library."

"I'm not sure if you know, you probably do, but ABA in

Hebrew means dad, father, like my dad is my Aba, that's what I call him.

I've a feeling that one day will be there in your old hometown, maybe doing some shopping, we'll walk past that library having just read all this again, and think, how strange, is AC trying to tell us something?"

"Let's enjoy the ride. It's a jumping off point. Might need some serious reframing, reinterpretation, but I'm not going to complain if this demon wants to help or offer information. Reminds me, a long time ago, I asked a friend, in part as a chat up, why did women find him so attractive, given all the negatives, and she said it was likely all down to his lack of inhibition ... and his love of yoni-puja, which you know means cunnilingus!

He was a charlatan and magus, a 'wise man & the fool', which I must admit I thought was a traditional Jewish circle dance, until you put me right. The 'Wise man and the Palm Tree'. Let's just take what is useful. The chaos magick we both love and that owes some sort of debt to Crowley, we will use it. He will keep us on track:

> I believe in one secret and ineffable Lord; and in one Star in the Company of Stars of whose fire we are created, and to which we shall return;
>
> And in one Father of Life, Mystery of Mystery, in His name Chaos, the sole vice-regent of the Sun upon the Earth;
>
> And in one Air the nourisher of all that breathes.

And I believe in one Earth, the Mother of us all, and in one Womb wherein all men are begotten, and wherein they shall rest, Mystery of Mystery, in Her name BABALON. And I believe in the Serpent and the Lion, Mystery of Mystery, in His name BAPHOMET. And I believe in one Gnostic and Universal Church of Light, Life, Love and Liberty, the Word of whose Law is Thelema. And I believe in the communion of Saints. And, forasmuch as meat and drink are transmuted in us daily into spiritual substance, I believe in the Miracle of the Mass. And I confess one Baptism of Wisdom whereby we accomplish the Miracle of Incarnation. And I confess my life one, individual, and eternal that was, and is, and is to come.'"

More On Aleister Crowley

"He is very active today ... is he invited tonight?

Coincidentally, I just read this passage in Michael Ende's *The Neverending Story*:

> 'Bastian had shown the lion the inscription on the reverse side of the Gem.
>
> "What do you suppose it means?" he asked. "'DO WHAT YOU WISH.' That must mean I can do anything I feel like. Don't you think so?"
>
> All at once Grograman's face looked alarmingly grave, and his eyes glowed.
>
> 'No,' he said in his deep, rumbling voice. 'It means that you must do what you really and truly

want. And nothing is more difficult.' "

"Lovely, when a passage jumps out at you from a book like that. I wonder if he knew this one from Aleister Crowley's Liber II : 'From these considerations it should be clear that "DO WHAT THOU WILT" does not mean "Do what you like." It is the apotheosis of Freedom; but it is also the strictest possible bond. Do what thou wilt—then do nothing else. Let nothing deflect thee from that austere and holy task. Liberty is absolute to do thy will; but seek to do any other thing whatever, and instantly obstacles must arise. Every act that is not in the definite course of that one orbit is erratic, an hindrance. Will must not be two, but one."

"Can you Explain it the way you see and understand it. Do you live by this rule?"

"I'm a slouch, but it's an ideal, like gnosis, the personal quest to try and find meaning and purpose in life. For me it is a religious thing, but not fanatically so but I've not given up. It is magic, but as it says, more complicated than doing what you want ... I like the Crowley disciple who said somewhere that it can even be thinking, or doing things for the common good."

"Good answer."

"It's funny, I didn't think of myself as very *into* Crowley, but I guess I must be, if it's that obvious. The old man probably wants to remind me or is it us? Sometimes I think I've moved beyond Crowley because I'm not part of the organised Orders who do all that. I'm an outsider."

"I think that's what he wants, is for all the Orders to end up in chaos. It is funny that I know nearly nothing of him, well I know a little more since we started talking about him, and I feel that somehow I get him, or what he wants now, without reading any of his books. I don't think he is worse than any other crazy cult leader, but definitely shines brighter than most."

"At least with Crowley his many faults are obvious, which in my opinion is a good quality in a guru. I think you can work it out without reading more books. Although one day, you might just want to do a little more reading. I think he would have, he does, approve of what we do, would applaud our more intuitive approach. The sexual magic thing, that was his big breakthrough, a simplification of magick but that soon got more complex again. His 'Scarlet women', they all understood it better than he did really, and they try to tell him, but he wouldn't listen. They called him out when they saw how he had failed them, and the work."

"What was the project?"

"Not sure I remember enough to explain. Those women, they gave up everything, and committed themselves to a new vision. He made them his priestesses, what he called his 'scarlet women'. and they embraced that role fully. But then human nature comes into play, or his nature, he soon tired of them, he was lazy, and drunk. He was like a kid in a candy store, he wanted other priestesses, fresh meat. Leah Hirsig felt he was failing the current when he embraced younger, more attractive woman; she thought he was wasting her, and her capacity to incarnate, to be Babalon. I like the fact that even after her split from Crowley, she continued with her quest for True Will. But these days she is totally forgotten."

"The 'guru syndrome' ... followers losing themselves for the guru, silly really ... doesn't seem like the way a Scarlet Woman should be, blindly following anyone. Did she find it, her true will? What did she do?"

"I don't recall exactly, something obscure. Spiritual women's stories, often untold, publishing them has always been a thing for me, perhaps I will publish hers. I think she tried to work with other initiates who'd been set adrift by Crowley and by the failure of the commune; they were all expelled from Sicily by Mussolini. She was for a time associated with fellow initiate Norman Mudd, although he later went mad and committed suicide by drowning. She faded from history, returned to teaching and lived on to a ripe old age. There is an, as yet, unpublished diary.

There can only be one guru? Given the times, it is a wonder any of it happened at all. Perhaps we shouldn't be too hard on Crowley for his lusts? He turned his own sex drive into the basis of his magic. Any magic that uses this energy could be difficult to control."

"Come and dance with me, I need to be quiet for a bit of focusing. Oh, and one last thing, send me a picture of your hands before we start, I'll send you mine."

"If one is going to touch someone in a dream, a photograph

of the hand is a useful prerequisite."

Stillness Ritual Session (19th May)

Mina prepared his meditation room, spreading a red cloth as a seat; this he did in honour of his shakti, Miryam. He sits, naked, but as the weather is still a little cool, he winds a thin shawl around his shoulders, which keeps him comfortable. He dances an opening rite, based on the ancient sevenfold ritual, the heptagramme – the four quarters, above, below and the centre. As the witching hour approaches, he starts the ganesh mantra as they planned.

"Om Gan Ganapateye namo namahah.

I love this mantra, I sat on the floor and sung along with it.

Almost immediately I feel your presence, and true to your character, you drag me from my comfortable seat to dance. We dance, exposed naked flesh touching. Sometimes we brush against each other, sometimes holding each other very close.

The mantra ends and the Stillness playlist begins. We have this method now, one that works for us both, a long recorded playlist, mostly prepared by you, music that tells its own story and takes us through. "

(Secrets lights – artist – Shir Sopher)

"I get the feeling that you are stopping yourself. This is very deep magic and the only way to become, is by letting go. Remind yourself all the time, I'm talking to you as a Morgan witch. To perfect this art you really need to let go, you are safe with me, and I know you know it. All I want from you is a kiss. The kiss is part of what we do and who we are."

"Unlike in the previous session, I just don't feel aroused, my lingam, it stays un-erected, resolutely so! It makes me think, I really might have overdone the cocktail of drugs!"

"I'm lying on the cave floor, on the soft sheepskins, letting my body relax into the sounds, trying to focus, sensing you, inviting you to come and join me. ... Towards the end of the track, I sense you near me, somewhere in the cave."

"In vision, I see myself sitting on the large bed in that cave that we so lovingly created. You sit beside me, we are cross-legged facing each other. Our knees close together, close enough so we can easily touch, so we can reach down, and feel each other intimately, as lovers do.

The vision fades and I am aware of my body again. I'm alone now in the temple room. I feel a bit like Osiris, as if everything has disappeared, eaten by the 'demon Crowley', who drifts in and out of my consciousness. Do I need something from him. Now I remember how, a long time ago, when first starting out in this magick, I found it useful to emulate his insouciance, his devil may care attitude to people, and things. It is my defense mechanism, a way of insulating myself from rejection or fear of failure. Back then, I found it helpful, but now, I'm not sure, will it help me?

Now Crowley is speaking to me: 'The trouble with you, my boy, is that you worry too much about what people will think, even what your shakti thinks. You should focus only on the work.' He looks at me, and sees my self doubt, my fear that I am not worthy of this task, that there is someone else waiting, someone more fitting than I?

But they aren't here are they, they weren't chosen, Likely or unlikely prophet I may be, but I was, I am! And Crowley, think of him, flabby, old and ugly, but with that unstoppable charisma, his ugly ecstasy. You have so much more. 'She loves me for my work ... She knows and loves the God in me, not the man; and therefore she has conquered the great enemy that hides behind his clouds of poisonous gas, Illusion.' Crowley has a point, he's right of course."

(The Flying Tree – artist – Native Zeevi)

"I stretch and roll over, so we hug, gently touching, kissing, hands over our bodies, touching, exploring. Towards the end of the track I get up to add some more incense. I light up a joint, and we are again lying back on the furs, smoking."

(Smoke Sign – artist – Bardo
(The Book of The Dead part 2))

"We are listening and letting ourselves go a bit deeper into trance."

(Hafra – Adrian Freedman)

"Still lying on our backs in stillness, smoking what is left of the joint. We are very relaxed and chilled, comfortable with each other."

"Mina, I say to myself, refocus on the meditation. The music has been playing I know not how long. My lingam had grown some, not completely ready yet, for that I need to feel the presence of Miryam's body. I am, though, now completely in the meditation, intensely focussed, tangible, like the colour that surrounds me, almost visibly purple or perhaps indigo."

(Don't Look Back – CMA)

"Still on the furs, lying on our sides, spoon-like, your hands slowly moving over my body, squeezing my breasts, my thighs. We are surrounded by the warm orange glow, is it coming out from us? We make love. It is the most sensual love making we did so far, you are amazing, your hands are firm and strong and soft, all at the same time. You are moving slowly inside me, I get shivers down my spine when you do that. My heart is going to explode. I love you Mina. you say it back to me. I love you Miryam."

"Time passes, perhaps 40 minutes since the playlist started our journey. I have a strong image of licking the intense moisture from your yoni, it rises into my mind, but then, almost as quickly, it evaporates. I shift position, on my back, in shivasana, which I imagine will make it easier for a Shakti to ride, though still my lingam is not stiff enough for insertion. But you know the secrets of Isis Goddess, she takes what is there and creates her own internal phallus, making her lover expand and grow within her."

(Inti Soul – Titin Moraga)

"Catching our breath, I get up, more incense, a little bit of wine. 'Shall we have another joint?' We are sitting on the bed smoking. I get up and dance."

"I come to lie down again, the playlist has moved on, and I've drifted into deep meditation, perhaps sleep. At last I have a very hard erection, and all the time, Shakti has been making good use of me, she seems to be in ecstasy."

(Riders On The Storm - The Doors (Billy Caso Edit))

"I rest for a bit, another puff on that joint, I like this tune. I have to get up and dance. I'm not sure if you are dancing too or just watching or doing something else. I'm totally absorbed in the sound and dance, into the rhythm, entranced. When the song ends I'm back on the bed."

"Somehow, through your yoni, you passed the vision of something to me, it is there, in my mind: 'I see five old manuscripts. I must remember what I see. Or as with so much else, when the meditation finishes, the memory will have evaporated. The five manuscripts are quite large and stored in a sealed cave somewhere in Egypt. Could this be the image of the cave as we have imagined it. The manuscripts we write are all stored there, in *loculi*, recesses in the yellow walls of the cave. Some of them have heavy bindings making them into codices, others are just lose papyrus leaves. I unroll one and read the first line, 'The soul of the sun is in the first line, the boat of Thoth is ready.'

The name Thoth is written in the familiar hieroglyphs, the sacred Ibis on a wooden perch, followed by the symbol T, for a loaf of bread, then the little sign, the determinative that means a god, a sitting man with a goatee beard. Although in truth, the Ibis pictogram is clear enough. Thoth, a sun god? Thoth is the moon, but what is the moon for the Egyptians, if not the sun at midnight. There is another sign, a boat with two lines representing a cabin or shrine, then a curve and on its roof, a disk. Thoth again."

(Tipa Shel Moudaut "a drop of consciousness" –
Sound of Light)

"We finish smoking the joint and we're lying on the bed next to each other, going deeper into a very deep trance. At the end of the song we are both hypnotised, the trance is so deep, we are paralyzed, our bodies still, and hard like rocks, but we are free, floating above our bodies."

(I Release Control – Prem Ardha)

"Still in deep trance, but we are back in our bodies now. We breathe into a deeper trance, releasing control. 'Breathe my love, The only way to really have me, is when you release control and surrender to the flow of love that will heal us.' I put my hand in yours, we are lying on our backs, side by side, my right hand holding your left hand. We are spiraling down the rabbit hole."

(Gaitri Mantra – Uria Tsur)

"We stretch, and roll over onto our sides,
facing each other.
We are kissing, touching, licking, sucking.
You are inside me
I'm exploding into a million rays of lights.

You are moving inside me,
in a magickal rhythm,
with each movement
another star is born,
and at the same time dies,
galaxies upon galaxies
reveal their secrets to me.
I can't take it anymore,
you are thrusting in me,
don't stop please
I'm dying here,
It is too much
The Mantra is finished
both of us are exploding
into tiny beats of rhythm,
a thousand new suns have appeared
in our sky.
Stay, don't go yet.
Stay inside just for a little longer.
Did we die
go to heaven?
We hug and kiss,
our bodies relaxed,
you slip out."

"All the while, Shakti has been astride me, in ecstasy, one orgasm following another. Now I too am beyond the point of no return, I will come soon, I've waited so long but I know my Miryam wants to feel the fountain inside her. It is her way. I let it go.

(Totality – Intop)

We breathe. I think maybe you are asleep or meditating? I get up, drink the rest of the wine. Time to close the Umbra Zonule, the temple."

"After that, oblivion and until the morning when I awake, when the music has stopped, I close the space and return to sleep."

"I managed to collect a little bit of the blood, Not sure what to do with it. Thinking maybe to make some 'cakes of light' or a talisman to put in my medicine pouch."

Later

"Busy night – Babalon."

"I just got out of bed … It was nearly 5am when I finally settled to sleep. I took a picture of myself."

"I think you danced the entire rite by the look of you. I danced the opening with you."

"You could call it a dance, it felt more like we were praying together, one body in one of the most sensual sexy rites so far. I'm going to keep all these photos of myself after each NakedTantra session. In the one I took last night, I already look so different from the one I took last month."

"You look good, This one I think you definitely look post orgasmic. You also look so fit. I'm not so sure my photos at

5am would be as flattering. What is it you see in this new one, rejuvenation?"

"Yes. And something new in the eyes."

"The windows to the soul."

Lover's Story

"I invite you to smell my flowers and taste the exquisite taste of their nectar ... I can be your Blue Tiger Lily tonight."

"No sex tonight, not till Saturday."

"Tell me again what Aleister Crowley said about vampires? Rather you told me than him. I might be aware of a very long association' with the vampire?"

"Someone once told me that I am like a generator, I give out as much energy as I can take. Maybe that's why vampires have an interest in me, which is just like I have in them."

"Sexual vampirism is the thing I was on about. It can be a hazard in Tantra. Vampirism when it arises, can be one sided, to put it bluntly, one partner benefits from the sexual vitality of the other. And usually it is the man who vamps on the woman. Some older forms of Tantra seems to set up the exchange to work this way. It can be tricky ... There may be a physical asymmetry in the whole process. Let's just say, for example, that you have bigger pool of orgone energy available than your male partner?"

"I don't think so. I think we said already how we are 'like two fish, I suck you just as you suck me'. That way I don't conceive that we ever suck each other dry. I will never suck you dry. It is not my style. By the way, I've just learned today that Mar/Mer in Ethiopian means honey or sweet."

"Perhaps like *medhu*, you are the honey. There's a saying, 'the truth of my mouth, is the honey of my lips'. I know you would never suck me dry though I am tempted to say, it would be fun trying. I was more worried that, because of the energy differential between us, you are a force of nature, that I would drain you. But somehow I think we are both safe. I can't help thinking that the mutual feeding, it gives me pleasure to do so, breathing like two interlocking fish, in this way we circulate the *rasa* elixor, keeping everything balanced."

"You cannot drain me unless I let you and I won't, 'cos the implications of it would be devastating for you! Our fish are not sucking each other dry, they licking each other wet, and breathing and kissing and tasting the honey."

"You have the best way of putting it, we lick each other wet, and we make honey elixir, this too is what we feed on. And that reminds me..."

"Oh-o, info alert."

"Yes that, but there's a shamanic technique from Celtic world, *imbas forosmi*, the tasting of human flesh, this is a way of stimulating vision ... it could be same as sucking a finger or similar, a real taste to get going. Well, really the Celtic shaman sucked or even chewed on their own flesh. I'd say that's part of constellation of ideas related to ritual cannibalism, at least the tasting of human flesh. I might taste your flesh in a kiss or when my tongue is on or in your yoni!

There is taste of the sexual elixir, but also the underlying taste of the flesh itself.

"Hey, you are getting dangerously close to sexy talk :) and we are in purdah remember. So you will have to wait. But tell me more about this Celtic shamanic technique anyway."

"Try tasting your own thumb, not the whole thing thrust into your mouth, but the knuckle, the back. Or think of how it is when you lick the blood off of an injured or cut finger, first instinct is usually to stick it in your mouth! If a child will cut himself his mom will kiss it better and many times will lick the bleeding finger."

"Yes, the mystery of our own flesh taste, we take it all for granted, but one day, when I taste you, I'm really going to pay attention ! I'm getting sleepy now, will you curl up with me later, just innocent spoons?"

"Yes. I was going to say the same, I have another early morning tomorrow and better stop now before we start sexy talking. See you in our bed later but definitely not naked."

"Always naked !"

"We can dream of riding unicorns… Hey, was the mention of nakedness a little provocation, or do you think we should always be so, being naked in bed with you, it does make for a very sensual night, but guess I will get used to it. And those unicorns, 'riding on the horn of the unicorn', it has special meaning for us now, doesn't it?"

"What do you think?"

"I think."

"I want you to take me to that beach, I forget its name now, so please make some piscean plans for us to go there."

"Brean Down."

"I have an odd question, which hand do you touch my fanny with?"

"My right, just my thumb on your clit, if I'm inside you."

"Yes … kiss me !"

"Tantric kiss ?"

"Tell me how?"

"Tantric kiss, I'd take your knickers off to let the energy flow."

"I love that. So go on, what are you waiting for?"

"I slip them off, I can see your pussy, but now I'm going to kiss you, very long, my tongue in your mouth."

"Oh Mina, I miss your kiss so much."

"Me too, between your legs but kissing you hard, exploring the pleasure zones in your mouth, your tongue in mine."

"My tongue is wrapped around your tongue licking your lips. I can feel you between my legs. Touch me."

"Kissing you, my fingers on your fanny, opening, pushing the lips apart, feeling the wetness, sliding through the grove just as my tongue does on your lips. Your fanny is opening, I can feel the delicate insides."

"I want you so much. I'll lie on my back now so you can suck my nipples."

"I'm still between your legs, which fall open like the letter M. I'm sucking your nipples, my cock enters inside you, I can't stop it."

"Don't stop it. I want to feel you moving inside me. Fuck me, Kiss me, Fuck me and kiss me."

"Every time I suck your nipples you twitch in your fanny. I can feel you, even as I thrust in you, so tight around me. I'm fucking you, delicious long in and out, all-night now, we have to dream it."

"It's going to be my dream, fucking and kissing you."

"I think it's going to be mine too !"

"Still hard inside you but you know."

"Time to rest, sleep and merge."

Chapter 7
Transition

Crowley again

"I had another bad nightmare last nite, the classic ghost thing, pulling the covers off me, strangers downstairs. I call for help, then I woke up shouting. This is all trademark *akhw* spirit stuff."

" 'Pulling the covers off you ... People downstairs...' The way I see it, your unconscious is trying to tell you something. I've got a feeling that Crowley is lurking somewhere around

... back again after last time when he presented me with the fool.

Changing the subject, tomorrow, for the ritual, what do we do? At midnight?"

"Yes, a quiet time here for meditation trance."

"I think the playlist will again be 'Stillness', so download it if you need to."

Seth, Apophis & Baphomet

"I just wanted to say, the god, Baphomet, he often comes to me, even now."

"Tell me more about it. To my mind, Baphomet is like Amun-Min-Ra so-called 'the goat of Mendes'. So, using a bit of convoluted logic, our friend Seth could be an emanation of him. Both gods are thought to be together at twilight, just before dawn or as the sun goes down. This is a good time for rites of the sun."

"For me, Baphomet is all things of nature, and nature is androgynous. Androgyny is not just about sexual orientation, it's the way you think, it's the equilibrium of everything, of the mind, heart and soul. Baphomet is invoked every time I take ayahuasca, this was so, even before my first formal invocation and initiation. Maybe that's why I no longer feel the need to invoke Hir, sHe[1] is in my DNA.

I read my invocation again last night, it was a bit mad, I remember, when I came round, I texted a friend and all I could

---

1   See *The Book of Baphomet* by Julian Vayne & Nikki Wyrd

say is 'Fucking Baphomet' ... He said, yes, that's Baphomet, and we laughed. I had some mad ayahuasca sessions with Baphomet at my side, or watching, or just showing me stuff, in Hir crazy ways.

Few years ago, I had a vision about a goat, it was one of my old goats, I used to keep goats, it told me that my sacrifice has been accepted. The relation to Baphomet, it was natural to me, I suppose that's how you feel towards Seth?"

"Seth was always a mystery to me too, even now, maybe that's the attraction, and although I cannot see you, I can totally see Baphomet in you. It makes me dream of shakti in strange clothing."

"You called me 'a force of nature '... it's the Baphomet essence in me you sense. Seth and Baphomet, I'm sure they have lots in common. What type of clothing?"

"For clothing, I'd say try a cloak of shiny raven feathers or leggings, like the god Pan would wear, but not covering your sex too tightly, so you can reveal yourself when you feel the need. Naked is usually more comfortable. You are a force of nature, very strong, you make me swoon with your power sometimes, well, if you allow for a slight hyperbole. Tell me more of the Apophis club, obviously a big influence, did you ever stop."

"The Apophis Club was an online learning place about Apophis, Seth, Draconian Magic, that kind of thing. Full of great minds, altogether a great working and learning experience. It reminded me of my roots in shamanism. What

I learned in the Apophis club is that Seth is the initiator of unique and original thought."

"Seth and Apophis seem like entirely different entities to me. A while back, I was actually asked not to create any liturgy for Apophis, it would need creating as actually, there is none that has survived from the past, nothing not completely negative. In the myths your learnt, do you see Seth as a minor aspect of Apophis, or are they synonymous? You seem to know a lot about Apophis? He, or is it she, a very scary entity?"

"I know nothing of that ... It was a platform for me to perfect my skills and gifts, to meet others and go on the Baphomet journey. She is powerful. When you learn to open the eye, and you look into it, you make a quantum leap, very much as in ayahuasca ceremonies, that's why I got so into it. It was very familiar to me, even though the practice, which I found fascinating, was done differently, and not with ayahuasca.

I suppose I was taught that Seth was *mench* enough to look Apophis in the eye, and jump into it. The void is so full of opportunities. To jump in, you need to look Apophis in the eye, as Seth did."

"You're right, Seth has power of the eye, like Apophis, who must never be killed, merely pinned down, in the same way as Seth must be chained to a post at the centre of the mill. It was Seth's consort Ipet who did this to him."

"The way I see it, Apophis is Seth. Every night he has to counter the darkness, to kill it, the night, and by doing so, he masters the void, and thus, has all possibilities in his hands. He is brave really, going against all the odds. I think it was in the Apophis Club, I actually understood for the first time a little bit of Seth. Michael Kelly's conjuration, the one I translated, is beautiful. When I translated it, it was like I was possessed ... it was automatic writing, and it came out so beautifully in Hebrew, like I'm doing translation work all my life. There is one bit in your book I might translate one day, the poem with which you put a spell on me, 'Ode to the Cock And Fanny'.

"I'd like that very much. You know, come to think of it, because of the change of pole star over time, as the celestial mill turns, Seth takes over the role once held by the constellation Draco. All these stars mirror deep stuff in our minds, that's what I think, and I suspect that's where we are all going."

"Is that why Seth is related to Draconian magic? In ayahuasca, the greatest fear is to look the snake (Apophis?) in the eye, and when you do that, let her swallow you up. You cross a bridge, where there is no way back, hence comes the realisation of knowledge, infinity, wisdom and magic. Seth did that too?"

"Yes I think so. There is something else that happens at the end of Egyptian history, in which the two myths coalesce, but yes, mostly it is the old star religion that brings Seth and Apophis together. The interplay between the constellations Draco and Ursa major, over a very long cycle in prehistory, the so called nameless aeon, where the people of Apophis and those of Seth perhaps shared an ancient secret. It makes me think, the pole star, it is like an eye. This is all deep ancestral stuff."

"I always thought about them as one, something like a mutual reflection of Seth or Apophis in a mirror. You say Apophis has the power of the 'evil' eye, the way I see it, he just has the power of the eye, period, the all seeing eye and everything, whatever, that comes with it."

"The dream tonight will be about doors and going through them. You have the key, you just need to remember you've got it as you are dreaming. There is a special room or terrace where we meet, our pleasure palace for eternity. You just have to go through first, I'll meet you on the other side of the 'false' door. Once you enter the darkness of the square door there is nothing. The deeper you go, there will be more light or space around you, deeper still, and you'll find the source, which is made of triangles and round shapes. But if you look carefully, right in the middle, you'll see it all again."

More on ritual

"What should a magic ring of power look like? When we touch each other, or do the 69 or yabyum or baboons crouching, this is our magick circle.

Think of the Fool, he is also the circle. We are the circle. When we physically connect, we create it, when we separate, we close the circle."

"The number of the fool is 0, which has the energy of the ouroboros serpent, eating its own tail. He is the kiss, the magical cycle of the breath of life ritual. The Fool = Zero in the sequence, thus it corresponds with the Hebrew letter Aleph. The element of air, and the planet Uranus. Aleph I think has no sound value of its own, but takes on the sound of the vowel that accompanies it."

"Aleph when spelt out is Aleph, Lamed, Pe. Reverse this (Aleph) אלם and it becomes Pele פלא, meaning magic or a wonder."

"Which perhaps is something to do with English, actually Cornish Pela, meaning cunning man, witch or exorcist."

"The fool is the beginning of a journey into the fractal world, the black dot in any such shape, the world inside a world and so on to infinity. In terms of the Tarot, each Atu is another step taken further down the path …

Mina, you know me by now, I'm not very ritualistic. My style is minimalist, most of the time I don't even use an altar, or 'my body is the altar'. Sound vibrations work very well for me, which is why I love the Gnostic Pentagram Rite. Sometimes I add Tibetan singing bowls, not too many gestures, and only when they are spontaneous. Part of my 'initiation' into chaos magic and chaos craft was to learn those vibrations, each one of which represents one of the Chaos spheres."

Hippo/Tawaret, and the nature of Transition

"I have an idea concerning Ipet, the Hippo goddess, the one who tethers Seth, perhaps the theme is to be one of release?"

"Seth is really tethered? So, in the ritual, you would be Seth, and I'm the Hippo goddess, we are gazing into each other's eyes, and then we see what comes from that?"

"In the myth, Seth is said to be tethered to the polestar, either by Tawaret the Hippo goddess, or she holds him there, or he is tied to her."

"Seth is inside the Hippo?"

"Well, I suppose it could be that way, they are quite intimate, could even be a tantric vibe there. She is thought of as one of his 'consorts'. Sometimes she is the Polestar, around which he revolves."

"He does like his beasts ... Remember I'm your Baphomet, things could get pretty wild. I can be the wildest beast you always dreamt about, are you ready for that? Did the lioness Sekhmet have anything to do with Seth?"

"A ferocious hippo is obviously right for you then. Follow the logic of the myth, is all I can say. Seth will be your match in beastliness, you are a force of nature. In the end, all these ferocious goddesses, they always have a benign side for those they love. So I don't think we will tear each other apart, but you never know. We are both piscean after all, we have dual natures.

Sekhmet, is another wild goddess, famous for eating humanity. It took the prospect of a good party to distract and calm her, which seems to be the universal way to deal with the savage beast in us all, beer and sex. Did you know Ipet, the Hippo, she is a doula, as you are, indeed as is Seth."

"Seth is a doula?"

"Yes, Seth, it's one of the surprising things in a god full of surprises, he protects the newly born, or those about to be born, as with the sun just before the dawn. The archaeologists found many amulets for this purpose, all with his image prominent upon them. He is always there at difficult moments of transition."

"Do you understand what doula does? Transition. You get doulas for births and doulas for deaths. Most doulas will act, because of situations, as a midwife at least once in their professional practice. A doula offers emotional support through pregnancy and labour. If both Seth and Ipet are doulas, but also they are somehow tied together, that's the mystery we need to work out. What transition are they supporting? Is it their transition? Or are they supporting a new arrival? So what we have here, is that together, they are to master the art of transition.

Last night I was going to tell you about Shifra and Pouah, the first midwives in the Bible. During the time when the Hebrews were in Egypt, when the Pharaoh ordered all baby boys to be killed, they worked against it by trying to hide as many babies as they could. Which is how we got Moses.

It's believed that Shifra and Pouaha are actually the names of Yochebed and Miriam, which are, respectively, Moses' mom and sister, who were both midwives. I think I understand what our next session is about."

"You do? Then you better spell it out for me. So come on, you probably know more about these characters than anyone else, help me here. Magical child equals a moon child? Or just transformation and transition in general?"

"The realisation, understanding and acceptance of transition allows for the transformation to take place, and yes, sometimes a magical child is created and born, sometimes it is us that is reborn. Only by going through the experience can we know for sure. Find a spell for transitioning. Maybe the *merkava* (chariot) meditation I sent last week."

Premonitory dreams

"My deep mind is anticipating tomorrow's ritual. After we spoke, I went to bed. Then at around 2am, I woke from a dream and the sound of dogs barking in alarm.

In the dream I had to find and save a baby donkey. It's tiny, maybe a miniature? It is so tired, and I can tell it's thirsty. I take it to a little pool of water and gently put it down so he can drink. I can see in his eyes that this was the right thing to do, and the 'thank you' smile donkeys have. I know it needs to feed, it's only a baby, so I take it home and I give it special baby formula I keep for the animals I care for. When I get home, Miryam is there! I know I'm Miryam, but in the dream, she was not me, she was there to help. Myriam was standing in the room without her shirt, her breasts full and flowing with milk. I gave her the baby donkey and she tries to feed it.

So I woke up to the sound of the dogs barking. The dream was so vivid and strong it took me a few seconds to separate the dream from what was happening outside. I can hear voices. I go out only to find some lads messing with the horses, so I set the dogs lose, who chase them away. Outside all was fine with the horses in the stable, and mine in the field. Even so this was all far from usual, as the ranch is well away from the village. Did you dream anything?"

"Yes, I dreamt lots of dreams, but most vividly, in the one I remember, I was very scantily dressed, maybe just furry leggings, like the god pan wears. I am performing, dancing with the audience all around. I lifted a great T shaped, wooden staff. It is very heavy, like the powerful Egyptian *Was* sceptre, or those T pillars from Gobekli Tepe. It takes all my energy to lift it, I struggle a bit before letting it crash to the floor with a great booming thud. I continue lifting and letting it drop so it makes the rhythm for my dance."

Now I'm with you in our tent in the desert, the sanctuary like those carried by the ancient Israelites in the Sinai, the place they say the divine presence appears. Together our dance becomes more ecstatic. We're both aroused, not caring if anyone sees us. You are dark Nephthys, sister-bride of Seth. The gods who were 'married in utero' and born as twins. Seth and Nephthys, the male and female ancestral pair, androgynous. We excite each other, my phallus is inside you and still we dance, balancing with the sceptre, spinning and making a celestial beat."

Ipet Invocation

Awake and embrace the void
Your heart strong enough for its joys
and its worries
Leave, and when you awake to life
You will feel young again on the new day
Rest, lie down assured of long good health.
"Good night,
the gods protect you,
their protection is before you each day
No bad thing approaches
The demon (Apep) is repelled from your bed chamber
Ipet the Great protects you in your long and powerful life."
The day and night illumined,
You shine forth
For she guides your steps on the right path,
And you know what is needed,
The god Ptah provisions you,
filling your storeroom,
With food and drink aplenty,
and in good measure.
Your diary and records all in order
and well composed.
The mistakes of the past forgotten,
The staff in your hand well made and sustaining.
Break bread with the wise,
Your cares all behind you.

Only reason lies before you,
The best is yet to come.

* * *

Praise be to TAWERET,
Bringing 'perfection' in her beautiful name.
I praise her to the limits of the sky,
I desire her Ka, calming me day after day.
Be merciful to me,
May I behold your mercy,
You, of perfect mercy!
Extend your hand to me,
Giving me life,
And granting me offspring!
Do not reproach me for my errors
You, in perfect mercy!
Even if my helpers slip up,
My peers still reward me.
I desire your great strength,
None knows you as I do;
I will say to the children and children's children:
Thee as guardian before her!
Joy my heart should seize,
Because on this day TAWERET is merciful,
My house prospers with her blessings.
May she give them day after day,
And I never say 'Oh I have regrets!'
May she continue to give me health,

And my womb bear children safely,
[Or the future be secure].
My heart is glad every day, for sure
The good ones expel the evil,
And I am blessed.
Behold her people will live forever,
My enemies are fearful before you TAWARET!
Since your rage oppresses them
more than a mountain of iron,
Her mercy gives us life!

* * *

"After we have read this invocation, I start by meditating, before heading off into a visioning of the sacred place and the things we do there, until we have assumed these godforms, and can look into each others eyes. This is the closest we can come to staring into the void. I think so, or else the void will form around us as we look."

Memories of the rite

"We said we might end up letting the ritual shade off into Yogic sleep, what the Hindus call Nidra. No surprises then that the whole was very dreamy, sometimes nightmarish. It was all mixed up, as I saw us sliding backwards and forwards through the images and the timeline. At one point I woke with a start, something was really threatening me or us. When that threat came, I willed a magical word of power to come into my head, and there it was, I called out 'Runa'. This is a

Nordic word of power, so it seems a little at odds with this myth system of Egypt, but I accept it. But then, when I think about it, we can personify Seth as a bull and Tawaret as Hippo, or maybe Seth is also in his bull hippo avatar."

"A 'Runa' is, as I understand it, is a spell in the form of a song. So in the temple, it came as an answer to such a threat. I continue calling out the word in alarm until someone comes. Which they do, Miryam, myself and others, all together, the threat retreats, faced by our collective *baraka*."

"Mina, what you saw seems like the vibe I had later after the ritual. For the ritual itself, I went outside, walking around the ranch in the middle of the night, looking for our group of stars, and then, finally saw them. I stood between the horses in the field, making the signs of Apophis and Typhon, drawing down the Plough. The horses, they are used to my nightly strange stuff now. Note for our future selves, if we do this ritual again, it might be best on a new moon when the sky is darker. The moon was so bright, I found it difficult to see any stars. I could hardly see the Plough as the opening required, but I called him anyway – Ei IEOU.

I wasn't too sure what kind of music you intended to accompany all this, what scene you wanted to create in our minds? After watching the moon and looking for the Plough, I listened to Lisa Gerrard, *The Mirrored Pool*, which always makes me think of ancient ritual music."

"It was just around midnight when I danced and gestured to the guardians of the House of Life, to Isis, Nephthys, Seth,

Horus, Geb and Nwt, then finally the Hidden one. I did this several times, intoning the basic welcoming spell. I could feel you watching me already. I sat for several minutes before midnight, smoking some Blue Lily which altogether was enough to get me drifting in and out of trance. Again I could feel you there, touching me intimately, helping me get in the mood. I could almost hear you say, 'shall I suck you a little bit?'

That Ganesh mantra, it is so often our gateway, our guardian. I must have drifted away, because the mantra is over so quickly. I want it to go on and on longer, but it is already done. On my altar I have the image of the Hippo and a cup of beer.

So I'm making the invocation, imagining installing the Hippo goddess into you. Then into myself I place the parts of Seth than fit this work, sharing the common ground with him as he derides and faces Apophis. I recall how in the old myths all the things that Seth does, Hippo Tawaret also does, the god and the goddess, they mirror each other, just as we do now.

I sitting again, meditating, remembering how Miryam says that the circle is our connection, that when we are joined together physically, intimately, only then is our circle made.

So I stir myself, my mind switches to the place we share in our House of Life, which is also the primal cave. Here in the underworld, is a watery abyss in which Seth-Hippo and Ipet-Hippo connect. For how else will these two gods connect, being as they are, so heavy and lumbering on land, if not as they do in life. For in life, hippos are giants of the river, the river that flows down from the sky and through the land, the river terrestrial and celestial.

Only after trying several permutations can I get this right, and now we are touching. Seth and Hippo are indeed lovers, there was, there is a connection, but it wasn't always easy. When I am Seth my body keeps twisting and turning, and looks away from her. She twists her great neck and obviously wants to be kissed, but I am behind her, as two hippos mating. Seth, sees the folds of her vagina, and smells the heady essence of lust, still he keeps twisting and turning. You move your head so our mouths can meet and we finally exchange long bestial kisses.

Can I look her in the eye as planned. Now we are face to face, my eyes closed still in meditation, but I can't resist the urge to open them for a moment, hoping, expecting to see Miryam right there in front of me. Several times this happens. I see her face clearly but her eyes, I cannot see them, they are veiled, where they should be there are just the two black voids.

Back to meditating again. But even so, I again feel her taking me inside, encouraging me to see. I open my eyes and this time I see two full moons rising in each eye socket, 'the sun at midnight', the moment of maximum danger for the sun, when he in effect does die, only to be dismembered and then take on a new, rejuvenated body. This is also the time when the attack of Apophis would potentially be most successful. Hence our role as midwives, as doulas, aiding the sun through the process of transition from one body to another. Hippo goddess throws the limp corpse of a great serpent on her back, so he is pinned there.

I sense Miryam's question 'Who is it that is being rejuvenated, the sun or Apophis? And what is the new body he takes on?'

I reply to her that the sun god Ra travels through the underworld at night and at the darkest point, the midnight hour of the sun, when he is inside the body of one of the colossal serpents that prowl the underworld, Ra then leaves his old worn out body, and takes on a new one.

One final push, and I am again conjoined with the Hippo goddess, who is also you. Above us another eye opens, and a strong white light descends, bathing us both in the glow. This is the eye of the universe, which sometimes opens to threaten destruction, but this time for creation, creation out of the void. We are immersed in its light, it dances over our flesh, healing and making us anew.

As the light fades I realised how much effort this has all been. I feel quite exhausted, but make the final push, to wake from the trance. I remember the words of an old chant, they arise spontaneously from memory: 'vidoh, kaina poina panta – behold I am making everything anew!'

Both so tired now, still we linger together, bathed in the

light. What are we creating, am I transitioning to a servant of Seth? What of you?"

Ipet ritual but from Miryam's perspective

"I think it best if I just tell you my account of last night, and only then we might be able to analyze it and try to understand.

So where do I start?

According to information in Michael Kelly's book *Apophis*, the entity has seven heads, each one of which represents something else in the journey and progress to becoming, which in the ancient tongue translates as *Xeper*, or *Kheper*.

In my time at the Apophis club I invoked the 1st head, The Scorpion 3 or 4 times, then the 2nd, 3rd and 4th, but I never actually got around to the 5th and 6th head. [2]

The 7th head was something I thought nobody would ever go through with, that is to say, the invocation of all of the 7 heads. The 7th head represent the future self, the guardian angel, or the demon if you like. It also represents Seth, and sometimes it appears as a monstrous Serpent!

During the day I was cleaning and listening to music, and in between I was planning the invocation. The Typhonians have a certain way to do things, and I was never really into it 100%. I prefer to learn from experience, and my understanding of Typhonian invocations is that there is to be a certain order in how things are done. I don't do order. But in this instance

---

2   For more information on the seven heads see Michael Kelly's *Apophis* and *Grimoire of the Sevenfold Serpent*.

I had to keep within the guidelines for it to work.

So I prepared and by doing so, I remembered that to open the eye, you also need to invoke your futureself. After you open the eye, it is really best to call upon one of the heads. There is no point of leaving the eye open with no one to guide you through it. And I knew I'm going to invoke the 7th head. It is perfect for our session tonight. I was a little nervous I must admit, am I really going to invoke the 7th head? It's a myth isn't it?

Fuck! calling upon Seth, the lord of darkness, the Principle of Isolated intelligence, god of the Unknown future.

I started, before midnight with banishing, and realised I needed a proper one this time. So I whistle to the four corners, and then started. I'm getting a bit carried away, so I end up doing three different kinds of banishing, just to be on the safe side! You can take the girl out of the chaos, but you can't take the chaos out of the girl...

After that I went to the garden altar and lit a candle, burned some incense and made an offering of beer and some bread. I put the little cake of light in the incense burner, and looked up to the sky for Him, as soon as I saw him, I stood in the Apophis and Typhon posture and chanted the IAO for a little while. Satisfied, I went back inside and started with the singing and dancing to the beautiful Ganesh mantra.

The Invocation

Earlier in the day I drew the sigil for the 7th head and mixed

Dragon's Blood powder into some red wine, I never tried it before, but what can be more symbolic than drinking actual dragon's blood, especially when part of the invocation reads:

> 'Here I stand, initiate of the Dragon Mysteries
> And I am as you are, a void dweller.
> The blood of the Dragon pulses through my veins;
> My bones and flesh are of your substance'
> (Michael Kelly *Grimoire of the Sevenfold Serpent*)

This is so very much an ayahuascaro thing to say, when I drink it, one of the blessings prayer evocations I offer to her would be:

> 'Your blood is my blood
> We are one
> Blessed be and bless me
> Guide me through this mysterious
> and magical journey
> Time travel back in time
> Into the future, into the void
> A journey of passionate reflections.'

So I call upon my futureself and charge the wine and dragon's blood, and I drink it. It is stronger than I remember, the tingling sensation rushing through my veins. It's time to invoke the 7th head so I stare at the sigil and say the words of the invocation.

It is done.

Everything becomes quiet for a few seconds, minutes, dead quiet. I'm not sure for how long I stood there till I felt something behind me. It doesn't spook me, which is surprising.

Seth is present in the room, I felt him immediately, strong, stable and daring. Everything I say, he Is daring me to question. So I find myself telling him what needs to be done in a very confident way, not even thinking twice about it.

I knew what I needed from him, so I just said it and this leads to a bizarre conversation, which takes me to your question:

'What are we creating, are you transitioning to a servant of Seth?' I'm really not sure what we are creating, except for the obvious, a good friendship. I hope it will be revealed to us one day.

I always had problems addressing authorities, at school, in the army, to the gods. It was always my good luck that they recognize the naive-fool I carry around inside me. They understood that I mean no disrespect to anyone, it is just the way I am, the way I talk. In the invocation I just start by saying all I needed to say to mighty Seth, and for one second, I was thinking to myself, what are you doing woman? But it was like staring into a mirror, into the void? I was staring into the eye, and I knew that now is the best time to say things as they are, that there is no god, apart from that I am god. We are partners in this journey, I do my bit, you do yours.

I'm trying to think about how I'm going to end this conversation when he just says; 'Drink, Partner!' All the while I'm thinking to myself, yes, 'Partner' sounds so much better than 'My Lord' or 'Prince of Darkness'!

This might sound weird to you, but I let you into my head

now, and that's the way things are in there.

You asked 'am I transitioning to a servant of Seth', I'm not sure what this means anymore. Everything around me now goes into slow motion, at times the sound of silence is quite alarming, my heart racing and then the god says, 'I need some beer, so drink!'

I could feel you around me, my power ring, my circle. I knew I just did something incredible, but not sure what it is. We have some beer by the altar, then he says go, go and feel what it is like...

So I go in the house and listen to the playlist. I'm wearing my red dress but otherwise am naked underneath. I feel very comfortable in red, which for me is unusual. I feel very sexy. I'm also very stoned, my blood is tingling and your playlist sends me far, far away. So I lie on my sofa getting even more stoned and flying with the music. The room is pretty dark but more new thoughts keep bubbling up in my mind. I write them in my diary, like little messages, some private, some to share later.

The Playlist

So lying on the sofa feeling pretty good with myself and very much stoned. I try to dance for a bit, but I can't get it together, the room is spinning, it seems better to just go back to the sofa.

My mind is flying with the music, every now and again a message comes through and I write it down. The music is very slow and trancy. I feel like one does on MDMA, lying on a very soft pink cloud with cartoons pink hearts flying all around me. Bliss. Your touch is soft and slow, your hand under my dress, we touch and kiss and melt into each other. It is difficult to move much with a head full of Seth, so I let you do what you want, what I want.

You don't look into my eyes, it's like you are hiding something. Mina my love, I don't need to look into your eyes when I can see straight into your heart. I see love.

Sex on MDMA is pure ecstasy and we do that on the sofa. From far away I can hear a voice saying '*Wake up, wake up!*' I come around, it's just one of the tracks on the playlist calling me to '*wake up*'. I try to remember what I'm supposed to be doing, and yes, I remembered, so all these questions are popping in my head, things like, 'Why do you need this Hippo? Why did you let yourself get inside her and be shackled up to her?'[3]

Seth put a few ideas in my mind, do I fully understand what he meant? For sure, something to think about. Then the music carries me away again. You are always around me, I mean literally around me, like a snake coiling around my body. The feel of your body is so soft and warm, you know your way around me...

I hear a voice saying '*You have to believe me when I say that everything I tell you is absolutely not true*'... He is smiling at me and winking that eye of his, and then he leaves.

I wait for the playlist to finish, before getting up and

consigning the 7th head back whence it came. The circle is closed with as many banishing as I could remember, and do, being off my head and hardly able to stand. It is 4am, the sun is just coming up. I wind my whistle to the four corners, welcoming the new dawn.

It is done!

Red Mage

"So now we know that there is no need to release Seth, he never was tied to anything, when he is with Tawaret the Hippo goddess, he is there because he wants to be near her.

Mina, my love. I'm a bit overwhelmed with the events of the day, so I'm not thinking clearly, but I can tell you right away, that the seven headed serpent, which for you is represented by the Bull, has been awakened, as has mine. God save us both and everyone that is going to cross us in the wrong way. Knowledge is power, knowledge is dangerous. The fire keeper in me let the fire run very high, the fire goddesses are at large and furious.

And again, all throughout this week I've been brilliant but in a different way. All the information I've collected during my time at work suddenly registered, and I've realised I don't want to work there anymore, I don't like the way the place is run and I can't ignore it.

Thinking back to the ritual I remembered how the seventh head of the dragon we invoked brought with it the Red Mage, which is all about how to earth one's insights into the here and now. Today the Red Mage[3] is full on, I know what needs to be done.

In my day job I get on well with everyone apart from one; she doesn't like me cos' she knows I can read her like an open book. She's a bully, pretending to be nice, but she can't get her act together for more than a few minutes. So, I was sitting opposite her, and she asks me to tell her what I think needs to be done to improve things at work. And I'm thinking to myself, she is not serious, dare I tell her, so I did. She was so furious, I knew that if I stayed it would turn ugly so I just got up and walked away.

What really bugs me is the way she bullies her partner in front of everyone, I can't stand that. But I also cannot work with a person who will not stand up for themselves. I have stopped fighting other people's battles. I know my ground and I know who I want to walk it with me. If I don't leave… sooner or later, I will be sacked, so I walk. And now, I feel better.

Ipet, Hippo Goddess, she helps one through the trauma of transitions, like those we are both going through just now. Seth kills his brother Osiris, with whom he has a secret bond, but they are part of each other. Now he has to deal with the fallout. Ipet is there to hold you or us in place, to help you check your emotions, if you break the ties that bind you to her, you will lose control.

---

3   For an answer see Red Mage section below

Seth has a very strong sense of the elements, fire and earth. I'm all water and air. It took me nearly thirty years to establish the earth and fire elements in my life. Nowadays people see me as very earthy and fiery but really I'm still all water and air. So when things get a bit out of hand, my water boils and there are storms on earth.

A few years ago I went to a two day ceremony in the woods, a night ceremony followed by a day ceremony. At the time I was working on the 3rd or 4th head of the Apophis serpent. In that night ceremony, I got a 'lesson' in controlling the body. It's actually very difficult to control anything on ayahuasca, let alone your body, so it was a very frustrating. In the day ceremony, the lesson was in releasing the body and letting go. It was so simple and so clear

All night I wanted to pee, that was all, but I was stuck in a loop of bodily functions and couldn't let go. This raises lots of other questions in my mind, blah blah blah, trapped in a loop inside a loop inside a loop. The sun comes up and I hear my primeval toad croaking inside of my head, I can see insects, flies, bees, birds, leaves, trees, and flowers; they all come alive, and I see Hir there, laughing at me, laughing with me. I finally let go and could pee. I peed, laughed and cried, all at the same time. I knew.

After that, for weeks, I was like superwoman. I was brilliant, sharp, but also, I felt, burning up. My mentor, he said, I'm having a ride with the white mage. The white mage is your true potential, your future self, your guardian angel, whatever you want to call it. It shines bright, strong and fast. He helped me to slow down before I burned out. The White Mage shows you what you can do, but doesn't tell you how to earth it and bring it into your life.

"Carnal Gnosis"

"Miryam, after all that, I also slept and was gifted a lucid dream. I came across you in a queue at the Post Office! Naturally I went up to you and we embraced, kissing, which I know you like.

Later I was sitting in the house and I saw a whole list of special phonemes, which I recognised as from the PGM spell I've been working on. All of which confirms something I've noticed many times before, that even a cursory look at a magical text is enough to make it work, to activate it, if it is the right time for it to be activated. I will work more on that basis. To be honest, it's not the first time I read it, but never before did it enter the imaginarium so successfully. So for now, I'm drawn into the little story that always prefixes these old spells, what I sometimes call the prodomata, just that, and the sound formula, which is what the dream seems to be showing me. From the dream I have written and remembered O and E – as well as *Ouse*, but there was an entire alphabet. Here is the passage from the published version:

PGM IV 154-285 - Nephotes (Khonsu)

To Psammetichos

(Prologue)

'Nephotes (Nefer Hotep in other words, Khonsu) to Psammetichos, immortal king of Egypt. Greetings. Since the great god has appointed you immortal king and nature has made you the best wise man, I too, with a desire to show you the industry in me, have sent you this magical procedure which, with complete ease, produces a holy power. And after you have tested it, you too will be amazed at the miraculous nature of this magical operation. You will observe through bowl divination on whatever day or night you want, in whatever place you want, beholding the god in the water and hearing a voice from the god which speaks in verses in answers to whatever you want. You will attain both the ruler of the universe and whatever you command, and he will speak on other matters which you ask about.

You will succeed by inquiring in this way: First, attach yourself to Helios in this manner: At whatever sunrise you want (provided it is the third day of the month), go up to the highest part of the house and spread a pure linen garment on the floor. Do this with a mystagogue (a partner). But as for you, crown yourself with dark ivy while the sun is in midheaven, at the fifth hour, and while looking upward lie down naked on the linen and order your eyes to be completely covered with a black band. And wrap yourself like a corpse, close your eyes and, keeping your direction toward the sun begin the words of the spell, as you know.'

So we need to do that soon. After dreaming all that, later in the day, the image of a great coffin or sarcophagus popped into my head, I was sure it was related. Acquiring a coffin was a good thing, indicates that the end, whenever it comes to your future self, as it must, it would be regular and done in the appropriate way. The coffin was not for a person but large enough for a bull. Which I already know, such a coffin is almost always an image of prestige and power, and must be a good sign in connection with any of the gods and entities that help us with the work. So whilst I am not sure what it all means yet, whether we have to find it or just enjoy it, it seems to be a blessing.

Lover's Story

"Hippo doula – I like that. If I want to dream about Seth, what do you suggest I should do, think, or visualise?

"Look into the night sky and draw down the Plough, this always works for me."

"Ok I'll do that before I go to bed."

"Are you nude, shall I tuck you in?"

"You're very welcome."

"I always have good dreams in the nude, things arise."

"Oh I can make you rise …. and ride"

"I know, I won't ask what you'd do, we conserving, so no

sucking or hovering your wet fanny over me!"

"I can't promise that! Lovely horn you got there."

"You can come ride later."

"I will. Mina, in less than a month we will meet again."

"Enough already, I'm going to bed to dream, don't forget to draw down the Plough."

"I can make anything work into my magic if I want. Kiss me goodnight before you go to bed."

"When in bed we kiss to sleep, you on top for a second. Till then …"

"Come to bed Mina. I will ride your horn later when you sleep."

Chapter 8
Down to Earth

My tongue speaks from the heart

My tongue speaks from the heart
When I cannot touch you
Doing it with my lips
Saying spiritual things
My mouth on you
And in you, Kissing
My tongue speaks from the heart
You responding, as we toss the
Question back and forth between us
How I might fall but rise again
The next day, renewed by your sweetness

The truth honey on my lips
My tongue speaks from the heart
And tells of Hindu logic
Where a lingam is also a syllogism
And consecration
The mere touch of the yoni
No thing is more sacred
Time for contemplation
As the pool of love builds
The demonic initiation
What, death the only door to immortal life
Seth kills his brother
As we must now dismember
Ourselves, each in each.
A simple thought
As we lose ourselves
In the great sea
Beautiful Miryam,
She who prophesies
Speaking in tongues
A most wonderful feeling

Mina to Stonehenge

The bare facts, we met at last and we got on like a house on fire. All the problems I may have anticipated evaporated into the balmy night air. What I thought might be the end could be the beginning, but let's see. This is magick to keep and to remember. I am drawn into the joy of something new and if I ever needed healing, then this I have. Things are so much more than I could ever have expected. Events have delivered to me an alternative reality, another dimension, which I can never leave. When I left the house to begin the solstice journey I wondered if I would ever, or ever be able to return.

Miryam is waiting for me outside and we meander on the old straight track to Stonehenge via the ancient sanctuary of Avebury. Strangely we are a little shy with each other, or is it me, even after all these months of intimacy. But slowly, the barriers disappear and we explore the sacred landscape together on this most magical of nights.

Slowly, we walk the deserted old road, avoiding the many thousands of fellow pilgrims who throng the path direct. At Airman's Corner, so named from the monument to Battle of Britain pilots, we stop and share a spliff, another first together, which turns out to be very strong, stronger than I had expected. We are alone and both wondered whether we should make love in the woods, but the first rush robs me of all will, so although we cuddled a little and kissed, we soon moved on through the fields. We greet the moon in its first half and before we know it are at the checkpoint, an alien place. It's all too alien for me so we retreat back to the festival field to recover. Well me really, Miryam is staunch, like that image of Linda McCartney, shielding a stoned husband Paul at the airport.

We move on through the security, most of our things

hidden beneath our long black cloaks. I'm carrying a *kakhreba*, fairly large iron castanets, and my heart sinks when I see the guards scanning for weapons. Silently I invoke the lord of silence, Harpocrates, who got me through a similar fix before. And sure enough, we are through. Now I know the answer, how do revelers get musical instruments into the inner circle at Stonehenge: Magick.

Hours pass happily, sometimes with old friends, sometimes just together, before it seems like a good moment to take time out to rest through the small hours that drag, planning to return to the circle in the hope of a golden dawn.

Oxford to Stonehenge then Glastonbury

It's nearly time, we said we'll meet at 4pm outside the shop. I'm so excited to see Mina. Many long months have passed by, in which we pushed the boundaries of dream work and by doing so, we grew fond of each other and became intimate in ways that even the Morgan witches couldn't predict.

Three months, five NakedTantra sessions and god knows how many chats and emails between us. It's nearly time, Mina is very punctual, I better wait outside for him. Will he remember how I look? Will he like what he sees? This is us now, two people, flesh and blood. We left the divine avatars on the astral plane. It's nearly 4pm and I'm so nervous and excited and … there he is with a big smile on his face, My lovely Mina. One look at him and I just know we are going to be just fine.

We hug, I kiss him, but I can feel he is a bit uncomfortable about it, so I give him another kiss, just to check that he is real. We get into his car, I feel very comfortable with him, natural. The chat is flowing but I feel that Mina is not himself, not like I know him, which is a bit strange, as I know him so well, secrets that he shared with me, so why he is so shy?

We drive for about an hour and we stop at a petrol station for something to eat. I try again, we hug and I kiss him, I can feel he wants to but he is holding back. Mina, open your mouth, we've been practicing the kiss of life for so long, how could you forget? Mina, open your mouth when you kiss me! And he did, we kiss, but he is holding back, but I know we have all night together and tomorrow and the next day, we'll be alright.

Miryam, I'm not sure I will ever match you and your passion, your free spirit and wild abandon. But, in my own way, I fly. But, of course I was nervous and maybe a little anxious at the big adventure on which we were about to embark. Burning boats, I dropped everything and came to you, and even after all those months as two people with a single soul, I faltered slightly, unsure whether the real could possibly match our imaginal selves, even when it did. Your presence filled me with fresh new life and I was made anew in your image. And now, as I write, I can still say that after each absence there will surely be another ecstatic reunion, when it comes, there is a making of everything anew.

Stonehenge

We've been driving for a while now. Mina is more relaxed and very chatty, telling me his wonderful stories. He is opening up to me, we talk about taboos, the conversation getting quite deep, revealing so many secrets, I wish we had thought to record it somehow.

We drove through Avebury, Mina getting very excited, he is happy. I can tell it is very important to Mina to get to Stonehenge for the Solstice, he is very excited about all that. I am too. I never really thought I'll ever be there on a solstice morning.

We are guided, blessed and protected by the Morgan people. Finally we are there, so many cars, time to get organized, to ready ourselves for the night ahead.

I change into something more comfortable, somehow skinny jeans and a T-shirt don't seem appropriate for this special place. Mina is so excited, which gives me an idea. I hug and kiss him and I can feel him relaxing into the kiss and kissing me back, a shy kiss, but a long and wet one. I can feel his heart racing.

The way to the stones is quite a long one, I'm not sure, could be 2-3 miles. Mina finds a path for us to walk away from the crowd. We walk and talk. We talk about the stars, Sirius, Isis, The Dog star. We laugh a lot, it feels so natural to be together, like we were doing it for years. Which in a very real way, we have.

We arrive at the henge of stones where there are just so

many people. The atmosphere is good, people are happy, excited, everyone is smiling. I have to go into the inner circle of stones, I just have to. Mina leads the way.

In the circle people are drumming and there's a guy playing a didgeridoo, I just love the sound, it always takes me back thousands of years, back in time until I remember what we came here for… *Bring it to life and to light and to love.*

Later Mina thinks we need a rest, we should go back to the car, our sanctuary and return just before dawn. It has been a long day, for both of us.

Back at the car, Mina pushes the seats down and spreads a sleeping bag for us as a pillow. He relaxes on his seat next to mine. I think he is asleep but doubt I can sleep like that, but I'm tired, there is music and I'm drifting away.

* * *

The Rite

It felt like no more than ten minutes has passed as I slept. I opened my eyes and Mina's face is so close I can feel his lips over mine, we are kissing, his mouth is wide open, I can taste his tongue, his teeth. He touches my face and kisses me more, exploring, learning, remembering. His hand passes over my body, trying to find the way in the dark. My heart is going to explode. My darling Mina, I've been waiting for your touch for such a long time. I guide his hand under my clothes, under my knickers. His fingers are gentle and firm, he knows what he is doing and he is doing it well – ecstasy!

Hand exploring yoni, finger over my clitoris, I think I'm dying, will I go to heaven? All this time we kiss, our tongues touching, dancing, licking, spiraling inside our mouths, like two little serpents, mating.

His finger inside me, his thumb on my clitoris, a 1000 stars explodes in my yoni and a new galaxy is born in my heart. I can't take it anymore, now it's your turn!

I slide down in my seat and lean over his knees. His cock in my hand, hard and ready. I kiss it, my lips over it, learning its shape, taste, smell. Lips kissing the serpent, licking, sucking, tongue spiraling up and down.

Mina is so ready now. I can hear him, feel him, taste him, drops of ecstasy on my lips. Mina is groaning like a bear, he is ready. Now my vessel is full and I drink the elixir of the moon priest.

It's nearly dawn. We find our way back to the stones and when we get there, it's the most amazing golden dawn. We are one now.

* * *

In the darkness with Miryam, that very deep sexy kiss different to all so far. As we kiss, she takes my hand and places it on her knickers, and exploring, my fingers opening her yoni, as I have done so many times in the months before, and as I do, I discover she is wet with love, and all is well. She comes several times, although almost secretly, not calling out, but inside I can feel the strangeness of her yoni, like a snake inside, coiling and uncoiling, gripping my fingers hard and tight, until she says she can take no more.

All the while she touched me, perhaps to confirm how excited I am. Full union would be wonderful but cannot be in such a space, it will be soon. Your turn she says, I slide my leggings down and she moves over me taking my cock into her mouth, sucking and slurping in the darkness, until I am groaning in orgasm, my come in her serpent's mouth.

I stop groaning and I again hear the excited chattering of pilgrims leaving their camps to walk back to the henge for the coming dawn. We are soon with them, totally revived, rejuvenated. I remember the old adage that if you are refreshed and clear, neither drained or jaded after an intimate encounter, whether with spirits, human or immortal, then this is a good omen, of how it should be. If drained and tired, beware.

Together we hail the new day and the sun's disk rising on the golden dawn. We feel joy and liberation, huge sense of freedom, nothing can come between us and our magick. We know, and feel blessed to have found each other again, totally. The sun is up on a new day but its seems too soon to head back, although Miryam is tiring, she is so strong but I remember her day began long before our meeting in Oxford. When we sit, I wrap her in my cloak, protecting her, her head on my thigh. Soon we must move again, to reach our lodge in Glastonbury, only then will we fully rest.

But one thought from a future moment springs to mind. In sex, the existence of the soul is revealed, unmediated by language, and able to converse directly, one monad to another.

Glastonbury Romance

Hours later, around 8am we roll into Glastonbury and our room there. Both of us are very tired, but, with one thought in our heads, *sex in bed!* We really need to take last night rite one step further, but how are we going to do it, when we are both so tired?

Once we're in the room, Mina goes straight to bed but I need a shower, my temple, my altar needs to be clean and fresh for the second rite. I get out of the shower and wrap myself in a towel. Mina's eyes are following me around the room, I let the towel drop and look at Mina, he is smiling.

I get into the bed and stretch myself next to you. I can almost hear your heart beating fast next to mine. Within seconds we are kissing, my lips sucking yours, your tongue searching deep inside my mouth. Our tongues are again dancing the serpent dance. Hands touching, we are two snakes wrapped around each other.

I can feel your hand sliding between my thighs, caressing my yoni, fingers spreading my labia, rubbing my clitoris, my body is shaking with pleasure. I want you inside me.

You have an artist's fingers, long and soft. The way you touch me is like you are writing a new chapter in a very sacred book. Your finger slowly enters, finger fucking me. All the time, you never stop kissing me. I don't think I can take it for much longer, an orgasm is building up within me and I'm going to explode any time now.

But you don't stop, my body is vibrating, shaking. Don't stop, don't stop, I'm dying here! You kiss me, kiss my nipples, then you slide down between my legs and are French kissing my clitoris. I think I'm going to faint. God Mina, you really know how to press my buttons ... licking, sucking, kissing, finger in, finger out, I won't even try to count how many orgasms I'm having, it's insane.

Stop it now, I want to suck your cock. Your cock is hard and now it's throbbing in my mouth. I love sucking you, I'm really getting into it when you say, come sit on my cock.

How long have we waited for that? I've been dreaming of having you inside me for so long, it feels like some kind of weird and wonderful initiation. I'm high on orgasms, my serpent is fully awake, and moving down my spine into my yoni to welcome Mina. The serpent is hissing and twisting around Mina's cock, tightening and gripping like a python. The python and I are moving fast and tight.

Your arms around my waist, your hands hold me tight I can hear you say, Slow down sweetie. Your words bring me back, they always do, and we are moving together to your rhythm, a new rhythm, slow and sexy.

I'm breathless, tired and more than satisfied after so many orgasms. I know you haven't come yet, you are waiting, pausing before letting go? Why? Mina, you surprise me with your weird tantrik shit sometimes. If not now when?

Miryam, my cock-serpent is learning how to dance inside

and with yours. I know there's a place inside you into which I must burrow. Let's walk a little, then I'll find and follow the way, spurting inside you.

I roll next to you, we hug and kiss and fall into a deep sweet sleep. A pause, for now.

A pause ... my mind replays the drive to Glastonbury, you keeping us steady on the road until after what seems like hours, but it is still just nine am, we are in our lovely room at the Dragon house. Mina mucky pup, whilst you took your shower, can't think why I didn't join you, as we did so many times before, I get into the bed and wait. And soon you are naked before me and then next to me. So we hug and kiss, and it is just as we thought, in our dream world.

My cock is the hardest it has ever been and it touches your clit, it's all so urgent, we just have to make love fully now, or we are both going to explode. Then in an instant you are on top of me and I am pushing inside. I seem to have become a virgin again, losing my cherry, like the first time, I feel raw and exposed in you, as if it is still a little bit new, awkward, learning to fit my body into yours, so they may speak, each to each. You come, so I change position, me on top to explore your mysteries. You know, in my diary it says I did come for the first time inside you then, despite what you say that I was holding back as tantriks sometimes do. But memory is a strange thing. One way or another, we slept, until midday you said, obviously recovered, 'we're surely not going to sleep all day, are we?' So we went out again for breakfast, and refreshed, if a little tired, as a treat for the lunar priest and sea priestess, we drove to Brean down for our special thing together again.

Brean Down

We rise from the bed around noon, it feels so natural to wake up next to Mina, like we have done it for a 1000 times before. I roll over, very close to him and he puts his hand on my yoni, touching. I'm quivering and wet with excitement. His fingers are again exploring, sliding up and down the grove, rubbing my clitoris. Mina whispers in my ear, I want to suck you and seconds later his head is between my legs and he is French kissing my clitoris. I'm in heaven with all the kissing, sucking, slurping. Mina is very verbal, he is definitely good with his tongue too. I help him, spreading my labia with my fingers so he gets everywhere. I can tell he is getting very aroused by this ... I hold his head and thrust my yoni into his face. He is groaning with pleasure and I come and again and maybe more I can't tell. My body is shaking with ecstasy I don't know how much more I can take of that before my heart explodes, but he doesn't stop. Now sucking my clitoris, playing with it. His finger pushes inside me, very slow. We have different rhythms, Mina and I, but somehow it works and make it all even more sensual. His rhythmic sucking, licking and finger fucking, drives me insane. I can't stop myself anymore, and I'm lost in a tsunami of orgasms, and he doesn't stop. I don't know what he enjoys more, pleasuring me or seeing me losing control in a multiple orgasms. I can't take it anymore, and make him stop. I'm catching my breath, he comes to lie next to me and kisses me.

I love you Mina.

Eventually we get up and ready ourselves to go out. We stop for lunch and then drive to Brean Down. I'm very excited. Seeing the sun come up on solstice morning in Stonehenge was an amazing experience, but something about this place, Brean Down, makes my heart miss a beat. I can't really explain it.

We park the car, stopping for a coffee break before we go up the very steep path. Wow, this really is a very steep hill. Mina leads the way, I'm behind him, trying to keep up, but he walks so fast...

We get to the top, but then I see there's a long way to go till we get to the fort and to the house of the Sea Priestess.

The view is stunning, the sun shining in a clear sky, the land is green and the sea beyond the cliffs is a magnificent blue.

Mina is way ahead of me, I walk slowly, to take it all in. There are butterflies in my belly, the odd feeling that I'm back home, even though I have never been to this place before.

From the highest point we look down onto the fort that lies at the base of the cliff path. We stop for a break before the walk down. Mina sits in the sun, I sit under a tree. Daydreaming the while, how everything looks so familiar as if I've been here many times before. The trees, the grass on which I'm sitting, the view down to the fort, even

Even Mina looks familiar. We must have been here together before, I know it, but how can it be? I just have to get down there now. We bypass the buildings, all I can think about is the cave, the ritual place. Three dairy cows nod and greet us as we pass through the fort, it makes me laugh in recognition, even here, we have glimpses of Hathor, the cow goddess.

We sit together on the wall and watch the sea. Mina is full of wonderful stories about the Morgan people of the old times. All the time we watch the ritual place, we cannot get any closer, but during our time there we watch, sitting and talking for a very long time until it's time to go back.

It's a long way, but we don't care. We have so much to talk about. I feel so comfortable with Mina, so natural. I can be myself, without having to explain the way I am. He really gets me, and that is something so unique.

Every moment we spend together makes me want him more, thinking how we are made for each other.

We are back in our room at the lodge. Six o'clock, time for dinner, pasta Bolognese ... or a strange looking but vegetarian dish. I don't remember the last time I ate meat, but I eat the Bolognese, it's so nice. Back in our room, Mina reminds me that tantric people were meant to eat meat.

We are just so very tired. We climb into bed and immediately fall asleep. It is 1am. I can't sleep but neither of us want more sex. "Mina, make me a little J". Outside in the garden, smoking, we look for the Ursa major constellation in the sky but cannot see it. It feels strange, how can it be? He must be up there in the sky looking at us, pulling the strings… he's always there. Mina walks to the side of the house and I follow and there he is, in his full glory, Ursa major. Now we can go back to sleep.

Friday Morning

8am. We wake. Mina immediately jumps out of bed, we have to get organized he says, we need to go soon.

I remain in bed watching him trying to get things together, but hey Mina, I think, I can see it, your cock is so hard, what's going on? So I say to him, 'Mina, it's our last day together. We won't have another chance to do it for god knows how long.'

He stops and I can see that it hits him, the realization, that those two magickal days are nearly over.

He gets back in bed, we hug and kiss. I love the way you kiss me, so different to our first kiss, we touch, I touch you and you touch me. You are on top of me, it is all like a dream, or hearts beating to the same rhythm. For the first time we move to the same beat, and you say – Miryam open a way for me, let me enter…

I'm so moved with what you say, for the first time in my life I am fully conscience of my body and realize that I've been closing against you, squeezing shut. Now I am opening up for you. I really want you, my body welcomes you. Inside, my inner muscles open, making a way for you, opening like a flower, maybe a lotus. You enter, and we move in the most magical of rhythms. We become one. We are both coming, your seed rushing within me.

Writing this account brought lots of emotions up for me, what I felt in Brean Down, I cannot explain, and what happened on that Friday morning, was pure magick.

Lover's Story

Back home in the Imaginarium

"Miryam, how did we ever go back to our own worlds after that? Can we keep away?"

"I don't know but we did. Do you want to dream again tonight, or rest? "

"I want you to kiss me in the dream tonight."

"What kind of dream shall we have? It will be nice to wake up with an orgasm and find you next to me, or on me, inside me."

"I'll try, through luck and the unconscious, I've no idea how we are doing it."

"You're doing fine, when the time will come, I'll ask for another spell. We have different gifts but together we can do magic."

"It's such an evocative thought, in dreams you always welcome me inside, just straight in, just so sexy for me, you let me come inside you, I won't be selfish?"

"How are you selfish?"

"In the dream, as soon as you open your legs to me and show me your fanny, all wet and yearning, I put my cock near the entrance, and it goes straight in, it seems so natural."

"We could play for a while before you cum inside me. Kiss my yoni and stroke it with your fingers. That's all ok just as long you are inside me. Think, when you are there, it is the only time we are back to our original form, we are whole and androgynous again."

"Tonight I will lick your fanny, with my fingers inside you, when you are almost there, I come inside you too. Then I remember I love feeling you, so I withdraw and put my tongue in you instead."

"I'm naked now, and in bed. Come and show me what you know, what you like, what you want! Tell me and I will touch myself while you do it, what would you do?"

"Naked, I'd sit by your side and stroke your breasts. Then your belly, but not your yoni, not till you ask, yearn for it to be touched."

"My nipples are hard!"

"I can feel them."

"Lick, kiss, suck them for a little bit."

"I'm leaning over and sucking them, my hand is on your thigh, near but not touching your fanny, which is opening. Then up across groin to your belly, all the while as I suck your nipples."

"When you suck on my nipples like that, I can feel it in my yoni which gets wet and opens up for you."

"Hold my cock, I want to feel fanny as I suck. The way you're moving, it makes me think fanny really wants to be touched."

"It does, Yes touch it. I'll hold you, I'm so wet, touch me."

"My hand slides along your thigh and onto you. You really are wet with love juices."

"I am."

"My fingers run between the labia, on the inner lips."

"Ohhh."

"I suck and stroke fanny, all around, maybe going a little bit inside, in the vagina, where you like to be touched and you're moving against my fingers now. You guiding them over the most sensitive folds. Meanwhile exploring clit, wondering should I rub firm or wank your clit?"

"Firm. Suck on my nipples when you touch me, rub my clit. Yes."

"One of my fingers each side now, spreading the goo make nice wanky strokes of clit."

"I want a finger inside, fuck me with your fingers and kiss me."

"I'm pushing my finger into the slit, now two fingers inside you, like a cock sliding in and out."

"Ahh."

"I kiss you again then push fingers in deep and out, you love this."

"I'm going to come very soon! I love your fingers"

"Come on my fingers, I want to feel you come as I finger fuck you. I'll put my cock inside you before you finish and maybe we'll just keep coming in our dreams tonite."

"Put it inside me now. I want you so much."
"Sliding in, you so silky and hot inside. Wow."
"I'm coming Mina."
"Coming too... Ecstasy of union tonite."

Afterword
To Egypt?

"Miryam, we said a year and a day, knowing full well that we would have to separate one day. Part of me thinks the most logical moment to do so would be after our reunion in Glastonbury, which is fast approaching. Will our tomb be empty after that, like those in Egypt which are full of memories of forgotten meetings that never were?"
  – From Chapter Six - Vampires

Seems like such a long time ago, early in our relationships, before we were lovers, when we made a pact to travel together to Egypt, on the familiar trail, in search of our roots, in search of its hidden lore. There is still a way to go before the journey can begin, arrangements to be made, darkness to overcome, and ancient mysteries of another late classical culture, dear to our hearts, to explore. Several further NakedTantra rites lie before us, and some deep despair and separation that almost overcomes us, as we wait for our journey together to begin. With only one hiatus in our loneliness, relieved by a chance meeting at Halloween when we return to Brean down. Then a long dragging separation that very nearly finishes our connection, and that would have done if not for the oath we took, a year and a day ago.

And what about the red saree?

We haven't really explained how we got to that moment. We have to say, the genesis of that ritual lies before us still in the story, there is much to unravel before we get there. But on reflection it seemed to us both, that we had reached a natural breakpoint. The question remains, would we ever really be able to continue as in the previous semester. How, given the power of the physical meeting, could we really pick up the threads and continue onwards, with the same dreams and techniques that had brought us thus far?

At the Airport

I know, I know, Miryam says no, airport farewells are far too hackneyed. But we did it just the same. I just had a thought I have to share with you. First let me digress and tell you one little thing I remembered about Austin Spare's 'deathbed' scene.

"Get on with it."

"As his visitors got up to go, as they were half way down the ward, when they heard him say, 'come back soon, I have lots of new ideas!' "

"And did they come back?"

"No, he died of peritonitis that night."

"Oh."

"Well, I just wanted to say, before you go through the gate, that there is a great mystery that it would be obvious territory for us to explore next."

"And what would that be?"

"Time and space, the mysteries of the kalas, those lunar flowers that bloom on each day of the passing moon. This and those of the orgasm, this is surely where we must go next."

Appendix 1

The Archaeology of Sex

"It ain't necessarily so..."
George & Ira Gershwin

To avoid differences of view, which are more perceived than real. Because we are basically alright, we have a natural tendency to think others must also share our attitudes, loves and pleasures. Are these values, eternal truths?

With this in mind we might compose a brief history of sexuality, on the premise that it does have a history, has its ups and down, its combined and unequal development, revolutions and reactions.

On an understanding of where we are and where we have been, there is a possibility sexual healing. Is there a presumption in what we do that we offer an enlightened and healing vision of sexuality?

We view ourselves as deconditioned, or at least on the road to liberation. Does this not imply that there is a well of alienation out there in the wider world, to which we offer some sort of healing? Are we, even if in a small way, sexual prophets?

Sexual Repression?

It seems to be the case the sexuality has and sometimes still is the focus of repression by those who govern society, be they the religious leaders or governments? Repression is not universally the case, there are notable examples in history and sociology of cultures and societies that have a more liberated attitude.

Usually it is said that repression would be where sexuality is viewed as something essentially sinful. A primary myth being that of Adam and Eve and their expulsion from the garden of Eden. The Christian pastoral or confessional manuals, made sex into something that, above all else, had to be confessed. It could have been something that need be no real concern to the priesthood and could be safely ignored. But for some reason, sexuality is often seen as something that needs to be channelled and regulated by morality, in order to avoid its supposed anti social aspects, and in order to emphasize its positive values, especially in reproduction and the family.

In modern, more secular times, the agent of repression, so the theory goes, would be the secular state, which since the emergence, or reemergence of Capitalism in the 17th century, has continued the repression of sexuality, in the interests of, recreating a compliant workforce, ie one not too focussed on sensuality, but disciplined enough to get out of bed and go to work in the new factories. This is a theory, and not undisputed.

Some look to the Victorian era as a time when repression was obvious but it has been pointed out, with much validity, that there was also an explosion of writing and talking about sex in the victorian era. It was almost like a new religion, with its own sacred texts and prophets. But there is a paradox, in that the Victorians also did much to codify sexuality through the creations of many new laws and definitions. So whereas before, things had been more vague, in Victorian times, several new categories of sexual outlaw were more clearly defined. Hence, emblematically, the end of Queen Victoria's reign coincided with the celebrated trial of Oscar Wilde, and a general new wave of censorship, which did not recede until the 1960s.

"What is peculiar to modern societies, in fact, is not that they consigned sex to a shadow existence but that they dedicated themselves to speaking about it *ad infinitum* whilst exploiting it as the secret." Although, paradoxically, we have added to the discourse with our own account, the underlying motivation is one of doing the magick, rather than endlessly talking about it.

The other thing we might consider is how, or if, this stuff happening at a macro level in society, impacts the individual, if at all. Can the strictures of religion or the law affect the pleasures and truths of own bodies? Are one's desires immune from the interference of a repressive state or religion? In the privacy of their own bedrooms, do people just know things, as they have always done?

"Let me receive all thy manhood within my Cup, climax upon climax, joy upon joy." *The Book of Babalon* v55

Index

Symbols
7th head 201

A
ABRA 109
Abramelin 55, 106, 111
Abydos 53
Adam 151
   And Eve 238
Adiguru (primordial master) 62
Adulterous love 9
Aeon 56
Afterglow 72
Agathon Demon 35
Aggressive magick 46
Aghori 109
Airport 235
Akhw 54, 183
Alchemical 10
   Wedding 30
Amba 45
Amber 139
Amun 47
   Min-Ra 184
Androgynous woman 97
Angel 112
   Of death 55
Apophis 56, 184, 186, 201
   Club 185
Archaeology of Sex 237
Ashes 21
Astaroth 112
Astral travels 72
Asura 148
Auvaiyar (poet) 19

Avebury 219
Ayahuasca 51, 52, 59, 187

B
BABALON
   87, 90, 102, 166, 177, 239
Baboons 70
Balaka 90
Baphomet
   48, 54, 131, 166, 184, 185
Bat 59
Beer 54
Behemoth 136, 138
Bes 5
Bible 138, 191
Bisexual 118
Blessing 29
Blue lily 42, 53
Bolot, Xavier 9
Book 168
   Learning 81
   Of Life 160
   Of Thoth 162
Bread 54
Brean Down 181, 226
Breast milk 148
Breath
   Circulating 100
   Of Life 142, 145
   Opening the mouth' (for breathing) 127
Brighton 116
Buddhists 10
Bull 207
Burning boats 218

C
Cafe de Flore 65, 137
Cairo 55

Cakes of light 20
Canto De Nana 93
Capitalism 238
Carnal Gnosis 210
Castiglione, B.
   The Courtier 124
Cauldron 10
Cave 160, 174
Celibacy 50, 106
Chandogya Upanishad 151
Chaos 112, 165
Chemistry 90
Cheth 55
Chimera 57
Christian pastoral 238
Circle 188
Climax 80
Cloaks 217
Cohen, Leonard 31, 69
Crowley, Aleister
   55, 84, 86, 161, 162, 164, 178, 183
Cunnilingus 69

D

Daath 33
Dance 51, 129, 177
   Spirit 37
De Botton, Alain 9
Death 117
   Natural 54
   Pose 23
Deconditioned 237
Deep
   Magick 170
   Minds 45
Dehn, Georg 107
Demon 52, 67, 104, 148
   Crowley 162, 171
   God 83
   Lover 37, 68, 160
Desert 150

Dhyana 24
Digambari 66
Disclaimer 4
Divination 43
DO WHAT THOU WILT 167
Dog star 220
Donkey 43, 56, 192
Door 188
Doula 191
Draco 187
Draconian 56, 185
Dragon 56, 91, 203
   Seat 104
Drawing down the Plough 197
Dream 9, 101, 192
   Control 147
   Lucid 43, 149
   Mantra 35
   Mysteries 21
   Sending 42
   Appearing 46
Drink 204
Drumming 220
Drunk 168

E

Easter 106
Ecstasy 221, 233
Eden 238
Egypt 82, 174, 234
   Blue lily 42
   Magical Papyri 43
   Spirit Dance 37
Ei IEOU 197
Eight 113
   Times 67
Elephant 47, 136
Elixir 127
Empty 145
Ende, Michael
   The Neverending Story 166

Eternal Fornication 74
Evil
   Eye 55, 188
   Sleep 43, 46, 49
Exercise 137
Exodus 55
Exorcist 189
Experiment 104

F

Fading 115
Failed 117
Fantasmagoria 161
Farewells 235
Father 149
Feed
   The yogini 122
Felatio 124
Fellowship of Isis 57
Fire
   And Water 80, 102
   Of Azazel 21
Fish 160
Fisher King 96
Five
   Fold kiss 26
   Senses 151
Flame red 18
Flesh 179
Floating 135
Flower 33, 44
   Petals 44
Flying 135
Fool 108, 188
Fornication 137
Fortune. Dion
   Demon Lover 62
Free spirit 218
Freedom 153
French kissing 126, 226

G

G-spot 148
Gaitri Mantra 175
Ganesh 17, 30, 61, 122, 131
   Ganapati 15
   Mantra 18, 170, 198
Geb 42, 198
Glastonbury
   37, 62, 91, 105, 160, 217, 223
Glow 173
Gnosis 83, 109, 167
Gnostic 127
   Pentagram Rite 189
   Tantra 146
Gobekli Tepe 193
Goddess chant 26
Golden Dawn 222
Grandmother 93
Grant, Kenneth 56
Guardian angel 209
Gurdjieff's Meetings with Remarkable Men 107
Guru 161
   Syndrome 169

H

Halleluja 69
Halloween 235
Hard 58
Hare Krishna mantra 23, 110
Harpocrates 217
Hathor 57, 59
   Mirror of 45
Heart 72, 214
Hebrew
   Calendar 106
   Cheth 55
Helios 211
Heptagramme 170
HHH 85
Hidden 198

Sentence 111
Hippo 190, 206
　Goddess 190
Honey 179
Honeymoon 125
Horn 153
Horse 54
　Heavenly mare 95
Horus 53
　& Seth 145
House of Red Dreams 16

I
IAO 55, 56, 202
Imaginarium 103, 159, 230
Imbas forosmi 179
Incense 54
India 82
Initiation 21
Invocation 115, 202
Ipet 191, 194
　Invocation 194
Ishtar 111, 114, 116
　-Inanna 111
Isis 57
Isolated intelligence 202

J
Jesus 53
Jewels 159
Jews 107, 143
　Folklore 55

K
Kabbalah 55, 109
　Receiving 109
Kali 65, 121
　Mantra 23
　Yantra 92
Kama Sutra 125
Kameshvari 33
Kapila 148

Karezza 73
Karma 118
Kaula
　-Jnana-Nirnaya (Investigation of the doctrine 127
　Cult 64
Kelly, Michael 187, 203
　Apophis 201
Khabs en Pekht 17
Khadija 140
Kheper 201
Kibbutz 133
Kiss
　124, 137, 140, 141, 142, 154, 171, 182, 214, 221
　Of Life 102, 142
　Of Life Ritual 129
　Of the Yogini 124, 127
　Tantric 154
Konx en Pekht 17
Kundalini 23, 34, 60, 85, 102
Kzapakowski, Kasia 9

L
Lam 32
Lamech 107, 108
Language 10
Leviathan 56
Liber 83
　ABA Magick 164
　MMM 84
Libido 57
Limbic 91
Lingam 144, 215
Love
　Lover 90, 163
　Making 9, 48
Lover's Story
　77, 99, 133, 153, 178, 212, 230
Lust
　Wet with 60

M

Magic 157
　Kabbalah 110
Malkut 101
Mantra 114
Manuscripts 174
Mare fire 102
Masaylama 137, 139
Matsyendra (Lord of fishes) 62
Maya 25
MDMA 206
Medhu 179
Meditation 24, 172
Melech 108
Mendes 184
Menstrual 95, 143
　Blood 95
Meretseger 35, 51
Midwives 191
Mina 153
Miryam
　Healing name 105
Möbius strip 164
Moon 216
　Hidden 9
Morgan 219
　Witch 111, 125, 170
Moses 55, 191
Mouth 154, 218
Murugan 36
Music 65
Musk 139
Mystoi 17, 18, 20, 25, 32, 35

N

Naked 21, 66
　Tantra 15
Nana 93
Natha 63
Necropolis 150
Negiah 143, 144

Nephthys 193
Neuburg, Victor 118
Nidra 196
　Yogic sleep 93
Nightmare 149
Nwt 42, 198

O

Obeyesekere, Gananath
　Medusa's Hair 36
Ochre 55
Ode 187
Offering 54
Old fashion 94
Old hag 49
Oneiromancy 43
Oral sex 73
Orgasm 73, 156, 227
Orisha 87
Orphic egg 163
Oshun 87, 88, 89
Osireion 53
Osiris 53, 171
Ouphor 127
Ouroboros 189

P

Pan 6
　Rap to 6
Papyrus 145
Paranoia 45
Partner 90
Passover 55, 106
Pela 189
Pentagram 64
Perfume 137
Perfumed Garden 151
PGM (Papyri Graecae Magicae) 43
　PGM IV 154-285 - Nephotes
　　(Khonsu) 211
Pictogramme 65

Piscean
  Tantra 63
  Traits 81
Play 48
Playlist 92, 122, 205
Poetry
  Metaphors for 81
Polestar 190
Political 110
Pornography 9
Prana 151, 152
Pressure point 147
Priesthood 238
Prophetess 140

Q
Queen of the Night 51

R
Ravens burial 54
Red
  Dreams 16
  Mage 207
  Saree 16, 26
  Veil Mysteries 32
Redgrove, Peter 39
Refreshed 222
Rejuvenated 200, 222
Release Control 164, 175
Rite 220
Ritual 90
River
  Terrestrial and celestial 199
Roses 139
Roy, Sharmila 20
Rumi 80, 102
Runa 196, 197

S
Sacrifice 164
Sahaja (spontaneity) 41, 125
Saliva 99

Sanctuary 18
Scarlet women 168
Sceptre 193
Sea Priestess 91, 92
Secret 83, 151, 239
Sefer 83
Sekhmet 190
Serpent 187, 209, 221, 224
  Deity 51
  Goddess 60
Seth 46, 53, 55, 83, 184, 185
  & the Seed Goddess Hathor 58
  Companions of 100
Sex
  How I like 76
  In bed 223
Sexual
  Healing 237
  Magick 39, 41, 125
  Repression 237
Shackled 206
Shaking 34
Shakti 33, 96, 171, 176
Shamanism 55, 83
Shapeshifter 38
Shiva mantra 20
Sigil 65
  Magick 45
Sinai 193
69 188
Size 58
Smoking 172
Sophia 54
Soror Tanith 83
Soul
  Female 59
Spoons 180
Stillness 170, 184
Stonehenge 216, 219
Story
  The end 104

Strange Angel 124
Streaming 72
Superwoman 209
Svadhisthana 144, 159
Svetasvatara Upanishad 20
Symonds, John
   The Great Beast 120
Symposium 15, 16

T

Talismanic 44
Tallit 26, 27, 30
Tankhem 59
Tantra 178
   Hindu 36
   Magick 63
   Of Eternal Fornication 74
Tarot 84, 108, 162
Tawaret 190, 195
Temperance 163
Temple 53, 94
Theatre for magic 43
Thoth 174
Three Realities 9
Thumb 57
Tiamat 56
Tiger Lily 178
Tobacco 88
Trance 184
Transition 183, 191
Trilithon 55
Trishula 89
True
   Not 206
Typhonian 56, 120, 201

U

Ugly 110
   Ecstasy 172
Unicorns 180
Union 158, 222

Ursa major 187, 229

V

Vampires 157, 158, 178
Victorian 238
Vinayaka Ahaval 19
ViniYoga 109
Void 46

W

White, David Gordon 36
White Mage 64, 209
Williamson, Cecil 162
Wise man and the Palm Tree 165
Wish fulfillment 50
Witches 66
Witching hour 67
Women 109
   Know 109

X

Xeper 201

Y

Yabyum 124, 188
Yeats, Georgie
   Technique 45
Yeats, William Butler 44, 81
   A Vision 44
YEHOVA 55
Yemanja 86
Yoga nidra 132
Yogini 63, 66, 90, 121
Yoni-puja 165
Yorke, Gerald 162
Youth 136

Z

Zain 161
Zar 133
   Visitations 48
Zonule 104

The Palace
Can you measure pleasure?

> There are four gates to one palace; the floor of
> that palace is of silver and gold; lapis lazuli &
> jasper are there; and all rare scents; jasmine &
> rose, and the emblems of death. Let him enter in
> turn or at once the four gates; let him stand on the
> floor of the palace. Will he not sink? Amn. Ho!
> Warrior, if thy servant sink? But there are means
> and means. Be goodly therefore: dress ye all in
> fine apparel; eat rich foods and drink sweet wines
> and wines that foam! Also, take your fill and will
> of love as ye will, when, where and with whom ye
> will! But always unto me.
>
> Liber AL vel Legis I.52

"... Mina, I'm in the bath, can you please bring me a glass of that nice wine, the bubbly we got earlier, and while you're at it, fetch The Book of The Law and bring it with you too, I would like you to read some of it to me."

By now Mina is used to my quirky requests and is not phased at all by that.

A few minutes later he is in the bathroom, holding two glasses of bubbly, The Book of The Law under his arm.

In the last few days Aleister Crowley was again hanging around. I can sense him around us, the old sex maniac watching us in bed, on the sofa, initiating us into his innermost secrets.

So I say to Mina that maybe we should invoke him and see what happens. Mina thought it's a good idea, but as we weren't sure how to go about, we just carried on with other things, waiting for insight and inspiration to come. Only later, while lying in the bath did it hit me - nice hot bath, a bottle of fine wine that foams and The Book of The Law. Altogether we have the perfect conditions to invoke Mister Crowley. I love it when Mina reads to me, he's got such a lovely voice, so hypnotic that it takes me on a journey to the realm of imagination and dreams. The bathroom is hot and cosy, before I got in the water, I lit candles and added essential oils to the bath. It makes for a very heady atmosphere.

Mina is naked sitting on a towel next to the bath, drinking his wine. I take a deep breath and go under the water for as long as I can. I come out and take another breath. "Mina, please start reading now."

I put my head under the water but can still hear Mina's hypnotic voice from afar…

> Had! The manifestation of Nuit.
> …
> Every man and every woman is a star…
> Every number is infinite;…
> Help me…

I feel like I'm in deep trance. I sit up and take another sip of my drink. All the while Mina keeps on reading.

> I am above you and in you. My ecstasy is in yours. My
>   joy is to see your joy.
> The naked splendour of Nuit;
> She bends in ecstasy to kiss
> The secret…
> … and his woman called the scarlet woman is all
>   power given…

I have a strong sensation that Aleister Crowley is actually with us. Mina is totally hypnotised by the book, he is not just reading it, he is telling me a story from the depth of his heart, and Crowley is guiding him through. From my deep trance, I can hear the sentences he wants me to hear, I can almost see it, and with each line, everything becomes clearer. I feel so strong that Crowley is really trying to point me at something, but what?

> The key of the rituals is in the secret word...
> ...Bind nothing!...
> For I am divided for love's sake, for the chance of
> union.
> There is no bond that can unite the divided but love...

As in a dream, I sit up in the bath, still drinking the wine, Mina takes a break from the book, my trance stops, we drink what's left of the bottle.

I say "Carry on" so Mina continues with the story.

> There are four gates to one palace; the floor of
> that palace is of silver and gold; lapis lazuli &
> jasper are there; and all rare scents; jasmine &
> rose, and the emblems of death. Let him enter in
> turn or at once the four gates; let him stand on the
> floor of the palace. Will he not sink? Amn. Ho!
> Warrior, if thy servant sink? But there are means
> and means. Be goodly therefore: dress ye all in
> fine apparel; eat rich foods and drink sweet wines
> and wines that foam! Also, take your fill and will
> of love as ye will, when, where and with whom ye
> will! But always unto me.
>
> And then something becomes very clear to me.
> "Mina, stop, stop stop stop!"

Mina wasn't sure what is happening but he immediately stops reading, leaning forward to check that I'm ok.

"Yes, ... yes, I'm ok. I just know what we need to do now. I know what is the palace and where it is. Help me out of the bath and I'll show you."

As soon that I was out of the bath I take Mina by the hand and lead him to the bedroom.

"So the Palace is our bed" he says, his eyes shining while he pulls me to the bed next to him.

"No," I say.

We start kissing, tongues, hands, fingers exploring, bodies wrapped one on another. It doesn't take long and we find ourselves in the yabyum posture, kissing and hugging. I can feel Mina's lingam hard and throbbing trying to push inside of me. "wait", I whisper in his ear, "I know the secret of the Palace..."

There are four gates to one palace;

"There are four gates to the yoni - the two outer lips and the two inner lips."

the floor of that palace is of silver and gold; lapis lazuli & jasper are there; and all rare scents; jasmine & rose,

That moment when the yoni and lingam kiss, you've just entered through the gates and are standing on that fantastic floor of silver and gold. You move forward and you can feel the beauty of the little sparkles of gold from the Lapis Lazuli and the deep red of the Jasper, like drops of ecstasy of the memory of things to cum. You are intoxicated by the heady scents of the most sensual flowers, a scent which reminds you, the wild scent of the most sacred of body fluids

and the emblems of death.

And what is the emblems of death if not an orgasm?

The pleasures of the tantric body.

Let him enter in turn or at once the four gates;

You can enter in one strong movement or push in rhythmic motion.

let him stand on the floor of the palace.

The orgasm is near, you are almost there, remembering the silver and gold of the palace floor...

Reaching an orgasm.

Will he not sink? Amn. Ho! Warrior, if thy servant sink?

The tantric bodies are sinking into a ritualistic sacred orgasm. The afterglow.

But there are means and means. Be goodly therefore: dress ye all in fine apparel; eat rich foods and drink sweet wines and wines that foam! Also, take your fill and will of love as ye will, when, where and with whom ye will!

Can you measure pleasure?

But always unto me.

The goddess is within.

www.ingramcontent.com/pod-product-compliance
Lightning Source LLC
Chambersburg PA
CBHW011951150426
43195CB00019B/2895